Aaron Nierenberg

Thanx for being.
Part of "the team".!

Jim Cahn
2/83

Bill Morin

Parting Company

Parting Company

How to Survive the Loss of a Job and Find Another Successfully

*

William J. Morin and
James C. Cabrera

Harcourt Brace Jovanovich, Publishers
New York and London

Requests for permission to make copies
of any part of the work should be mailed to:
Permissions, Harcourt Brace Jovanovich, Publishers,
757 Third Avenue, New York, N.Y. 10017.

Library of Congress Cataloging in Publication Data

Morin, William J.
  Parting company.
  Bibliography: p.
  1. Employees, Dismissal of. 2. Executives, Dismissal of.
3. Job hunting. I. Cabrera, James C. II. Title
HF5549.D55M673   650.1′4   82-48045
ISBN 0-15-170966-1

Printed in the United States of America

First edition

B   C   D   E

Contents

The authors would like to acknowledge the entire Drake Beam Morin staff of professionals who have identified and developed many of the ideas that are expressed in this book. They are too numerous to list, but without their contributions we would not have been able to complete this work.

We would also like to give special thanks to Tim Lynch, for his invaluable assistance and collaboration.

William J. Morin
James C. Cabrera

Parting Company

Introduction

THE nation's leading corporations—companies like Mobil, Sears, and General Motors—hire us to work with people who no longer work for them. We are called outplacement counselors, and we teach ex-employees the skills they need to find new jobs quickly and efficiently, with the least possible amount of emotional wear and tear, and with the best chances for professional success and personal satisfaction.

Since 1970 we have worked individually with more than 1,000 people in one-on-one outplacement counseling programs. As leaders of group outplacement sessions, we have worked personally with another several thousand individuals. When we consider the number of outplacement cases that we have managed in our roles as chairman and president of Drake Beam Morin, Inc., the totals surpass 15,000.

We have good news and bad news about your career. First, breathe a sigh of relief. You will probably never actually get fired. To be fired these days, you must do something so devastating that your boss forgets everything he or she has learned about the principles of management, forgets the personnel and legal departments, forgets the corporate chain of command, forgets everything but the words, "You're fired!"

Most managers are too prudent to act so rashly today, and most employees have neither the corporate muscle to commit such remarkable sins singlehandedly nor the visibility to call attention to themselves if they do.

But take a deep breath, too, because the chances that you will *lose* a job at least once during your career continue to rise. You might be "terminated." You could be "de-hired" (which rhymes with "retired"), another word that enters the language when it comes time to separate people from their jobs. A merger or acquisition might make your position "redundant." A rubber-legged economy could land you at the bottom of an "across-the-board staff retrenchment." A new management team might come in and "sever" you, a process that sounds as though it were accomplished with a very sharp retrenching tool.

On one level, these new terms reflect business' preoccupation with fancy words. The thought of firing someone seems harsh and old-fashioned. But the new words also indicate that the business of finding, keeping, and losing jobs has changed dramatically in recent years. The "company man" of the 1950s has been replaced by the "me-first" employee of the 70s and 80s. Weeds grow on what used to be called career paths as energetic young executives stay in shape by jumping from one fast track to another.

In the '50s and '60s, people lived good corporate lives and married good corporate wives. (Corporate husbands would come later.) When companies said "Move," people packed. Today, if a corporation offers a man a promotion that is linked to a relocation, no one is particularly surprised if he says, "My wife won't leave her job, my children won't leave their friends, and I won't leave Cleveland." A member of the Class of '52 hoped and expected that his company would take care of his future. MBA candidates now learn to change companies every three years or fall behind their peers.

But as people make new demands and seek greater control of their lives, they find that they must also assume greater responsibility for the consequences. When executives demand faster advancement—and prove that they are willing to head elsewhere if they don't get it—companies must clear deadwood from the corporate tree or lose their most talented individuals. Convinced that it must become more productive and competitive, corporate America is increasingly interested in hiring the best talent available. This puts other people out of work, and, since this year's shooting star may become next year's burnt-out case, everyone's future becomes relatively less secure.

As employees raise "quality-of-work" issues and demand jobs that are rewarding and challenging, they barter job security. Companies no longer feel obliged to create dead-end jobs. And when a sluggish national economy fails to respond to the commands of economists, politicians, *or* businessmen, companies can simply no longer afford to carry unproductive workers.

This changing business environment has introduced outplacement counseling as another new term in the corporate vocabulary and made the service that firms such as ours provide increasingly valuable to the nation's major employers.

They retain us for a number of reasons. They realize that a smooth transition from one job to another cuts the incidence of legal action brought by angry former employees. They believe that staff loyalty and corporate productivity are enhanced when employees feel they won't be abandoned even if the worst should occur and they lose their jobs. People who go through our programs almost always find jobs more quickly than individuals who fend for themselves. This frequently saves severance dollars for their former employers. And in an era when nobody's job seems as secure as it used to be, the people who set personnel policies may even consider their own futures when they plan new and more liberal termination programs for their companies.

But what seems surprising to many people is that many corporations—or more precisely the people who run them—really *do* have consciences. Managers grow more likely to agree that, in today's corporate climate, failure on the job usually involves more than one individual. Perhaps there is a lack of direction from above. Maybe there is a lack of support from below. The problem may even be caused by people thousands of miles—and a couple of centuries—away: those so-called managers in Washington.

People still lose their jobs, of course, a fact suggesting that baseball isn't the only game in which managers are replaced because it's so difficult to fire entire teams.

As more companies decide that termination is a necessary fact of corporate life, they may feel fewer constraints against letting people go. If termination is no longer the ultimate form of capitalistic punishment, it becomes an easier type of surgery for corporate doctors to perform.

But one thing really hasn't changed at all: the reaction of a person who loses a job. Almost everyone feels shock, anger, and surprise, plus a psychological inability to deal with these unpleasant emotions and a host of practical problems connected to finding a new job.

Corporation presidents react much the same as middle managers. Both feel that they have lost control of their lives. People who have been with a company for two or three years feel as shocked as individuals with 20 years' seniority. Elaborate severance packages do not dull the pain.

What is different is that, if you lose a job, you can get help today. You don't have to go it alone. Your family and friends can help. Professional guidance counselors can help. We can help.

We don't presume to know what you think or feel when you lose a job, but we do know a great deal about the situation that faces you. You are unique. The situation you face is not. We know that one immediate response is likely to be: "This must be the end of the world." We know how desperate you can feel. We know that you need and deserve support and encouragement.

We also know that losing a job is *not* the end of the world. There are fates worse than being fired. It's worse for your employer to placate you, to find a corner for you and not give you meaningful, productive work. It's worse for you to abdicate responsibility and turn over the control of your life to a corporation.

Most important, we know that you can turn what feels like a devastating tragedy into a personal and professional triumph. There is no way to escape the pain and anger that accompany the loss of a job, but you can control and dissipate these feelings. You can act rather than be acted upon. You can find a new job, and it can be more satisfying, more challenging, and even more financially rewarding than your previous position.

The process demands hard work and common sense, but no magic is involved. For once, you will be working for yourself, not for someone else. Through severance payments, in fact, your former employer will actually pay you to find a new—and better—job.

If you plan the search carefully, and if you put the same effort into finding new employment that you spent on your previous job, you will find a good position that is compatible with your skills and interests. You will also gain confidence in yourself and create real security for your future.

1 * It Can't Happen to Me ... <u>Can</u> It?

Anticipating the loss of a job is like choosing the best way to be hit by a truck. You rarely get to test even the most ingenious ideas, because you usually don't see the truck—or the ax—before it flattens you.

Losing a job is almost always a shock and a surprise. Your boss, your peers, even your subordinates may anticipate your fate, but they may not pass the word along. And if they do, you probably won't hear them. People have an extraordinary ability to disregard threatening news. Your boss tells you, "I know how tough things have been, but your work really hasn't been acceptable." You walk away thinking, "Gee, he really *does* understand how tough my job is."

Frequently, when people leave termination interviews, where they have been told in plain language that they no longer work for the company, they return to their offices . . . and bury themselves in work. What has just occurred seems like a very bad dream, and they hope that, like other nightmares, it will go away if ignored. They are also trying desperately to save the day. "I'll show them," they are saying, "I'll work so hard that someone will notice how valuable I am and save my job."

When corporations hire us to prepare large groups of employees for lay-offs caused by plant closings, we suggest that the news be made public as quickly as possible. The companies worry that if employees learn that the plant will shut down for good in six months, everyone will jump ship immediately. We tell them not to be concerned. If operations cease on June 1, most employees will begin to think about finding new jobs on June 2 or later.

In fact, when we conduct these sessions, perhaps our most difficult job is convincing people that the plant really *is* going to close. No one admits it, but everyone keeps an eye peeled for individuals on white horses. Many people simply cannot believe that the company will actually take away their jobs.

This unwillingness to accept or acknowledge a terribly unsettling situation is common. Even people who don't like their jobs use them to define themselves and the people around them. We begin conversations by asking, "What do you do?" Our jobs determine when we get up in the morning, how we spend our time, where we live, even how we dress and who our friends are.

The harder we work, and the higher we rise, the stronger this relationship becomes. If we reach the level where being driven around in long black automobiles gets to be part of the job, the suggestion that someone may tamper with things becomes cause for alarm and a good reason to change the subject.

Yet a terminated iron worker is likely to feel just as threatened as an out-of-work chief executive officer, so the determination to cling to a job is probably caused by something much deeper than a need for perks and fringe benefits. The real fear is losing the structure provided by employment. Many of us will try almost anything to avoid that loss of control.

Most offices, in fact, contain people who make an occupation of worrying about losing their jobs. Anyone who must deal with such individuals has no doubt sworn never to fall into a similar trap—and may have even concluded that *any* act of watchfulness is negative or counterproductive.

Staying alert is not the same as running scared. There are warning signals to watch for, signs which indicate that your job is not secure. No one enjoys thinking, "It could happen to me," but business life is so volatile today that it becomes more and more realistic to recognize the relative insecurity of most jobs.

Understanding these warning signs lets you assume a degree of control for your future. You may be able to save your job if you discover that it's in jeopardy. A realistic appraisal of the situation may convince you that you don't *want* to save your job and may prompt you to make a move to more rewarding employment. You may conclude that you are in better shape than you imagined. But even if your worst fears are confirmed, and the situation seems hopeless, you can prepare yourself to take an active role in the termination process and not let others make all the decisions for you.

The Seven Danger Signs

1. *You hate your job.*   If you really feel negative about your job—and do nothing to remedy the situation—we think that you will be terminated within a year. Even if you try to hide these feelings, you will probably pass them along to the people you work with. Most of us simply don't have very good poker faces. If you do mask unhappiness and dissatisfaction, the only measurable result is likely to be new and unpleasant blood pressure levels. Something must give if, each morning, you climb out of bed and think, "Oh, no, I have to go *there* again."

Job dissatisfaction is the most important danger signal, but since it seems so obvious—and because it is so widespread—many people never consider it as a cause for losing a job. It also makes people uncomfortable, because it indicates that what they feel, not what the boss thinks, is the starting point for most terminations.

2. *You lose your voice.* If people at work—superiors, co-workers, or subordinates—stop communicating with you, your job is in danger. Perhaps you anticipate bad news and have isolated yourself to avoid hearing it. Maybe your associates sense that your days are numbered and are pulling away from you. Either way, you should heed the advice of everyone's high school coach: "Don't worry when I'm yelling at you. Worry when I'm *not* yelling at you." If you are no longer invited to committee meetings, if you cease to be assigned to tough projects, even if you find yourself excluded from work-related social events, you should hear an alarm.

3. *You get negative feedback.* It seems obvious that more than one negative performance appraisal should be cause for concern. If you aren't doing your job, you certainly run the risk of losing it.

But you may only listen for positive remarks during performance reviews and forget that the most important comments are the ones which are toughest to accept. Or, like many people, you may convince yourself that you won't be fired no matter what the boss says about your work: "He won't fire me; he likes me too much."

That's a very risky assumption.

4. *The economy is working against you.* The fact that you do your job does not mean that your position is secure. Automotive workers understand this fact. Many businessmen do not.

Don't ignore the company grapevine and other sources of information. Rumors of lay-offs or deteriorating economic conditions within your firm frequently turn out to be facts. Yet many people ignore even the most obvious indicators. The fact that the new product isn't selling or the knowledge that inventory is piling up in the warehouse doesn't alarm them. "It's not my fault that they aren't selling the product," they say. "I just manufacture it."

It may not be their fault. It may very well turn out to be their problem.

5. *You're not personally productive.* On the other hand, even if your company is having a record year, if you are not producing, you may lose your job. Sooner or later, the system will no longer be able to carry you.

Most American corporations share at least one priority for the 1980s: the determination to increase the productivity of their operations. To do so, they are demanding more from their employees than ever before and are not hesitating to replace people who do not deliver.

We counseled one man who, for several years, was given absolutely nothing meaningful to do and was paid $125,000 annually for doing it. He was shocked when he was terminated. We were shocked that it hadn't come sooner.

6. *You miss objectives.* Not only must you be productive, but you must also be effective. If you confuse priorities, or if you don't manage your time well, your position will not remain secure.

Many people simply don't function in the roles that have been assigned to them. They never figure out their jobs. They keep busy, but they don't do the things for which they were hired. They never realize that the boss isn't looking for—and frequently doesn't notice—those other activities. He thinks, "That guy is always late with his work." That "guy" thinks, "Well, the boss can't possibly be talking about me. Look at all the things I'm doing. I work 20 hours a day."

Perhaps not for long.

7. *You fail to change.* If you cling to the idea that things will stay the same, you will probably lose your job. If the bottom line in your career is, "I'm going to stay with this company," rather than, "I'm going to grow with this company," your position probably isn't secure. If your response to a new plan or idea is likely to be, "Well, I don't know, we've never done it that way before," you should be alert to the possible consequences.

Companies are constantly changing and evolving, not only when corporate shake-ups bring in new management teams, but in the normal course of business life, too. If you wish to remain with them, you must be willing to adapt to them.

These indicators don't measure goodness or badness. Don't assume that failing to change makes you a failure. You may be absolutely right to conclude that the new idea is, in fact, a terrible one. You may have lost your corporate voice because you raise points that are unpleasant to hear because they are uncomfortably valid.

But no one ever promised that being right would make your job secure, so you should also be aware that something unpleasant might happen to you if one or more of these danger signs apply to you.

Reasons for Terminations

When someone loses a job, his or her employer usually picks one of four reasons to justify the decision: economic conditions, job elimination, ethical misconduct, or poor performance.

Economic conditions that prompt companies to suspend or redirect activities are an obvious reason for many terminations. Corporate response to a deteriorating economic situation has traditionally included staff reductions.

Job elimination becomes a cause for terminations when companies refocus their operations, perhaps through mergers or reorganizations. Managers may eliminate jobs and terminate employees in the process. Economic considerations need not come into play. If a strategic planning decision does away with a division, for instance, or if a management study shows that certain jobs are duplicated within the organization, people are frequently terminated.

Ethical misconduct—it is also called "cause"—includes such acts as breaking laws or violating company policies. Individuals who misrepresent themselves or their work may be fired for cause. Responsible companies typically deal with these situations forcefully, since failure to act may be interpreted by others within the organization as unstated approval of questionable conduct.

Poor performance is the fourth general reason for termination. Unsatisfactory performance appraisals, missed objectives or deadlines, low efficiency ratings and other indicators of substandard performance are included in this category. Poor performance is not necessarily synonymous with incompetence. Bad attitude, poor management or supervision, even antiquated equipment or peer pressure can create performance-related problems that lead to terminations.

There is also a fifth reason for terminating people, one which generally isn't discussed publicly, but which is certainly as important as any of the others.

We call it "personal chemistry," a term that refers to a variety of problems that can occur as people interact with each other in a work environment. Chemical reasons for termination usually involve problems in communication or differences in personal and professional styles. When managers say, "He just doesn't seem to be a member of the team anymore," or, "I can't communicate with her anymore," or, "He always seems to be confused," or, "She just doesn't understand the new direction we're taking," they are describing chemical problems. (By the time the individual gets the bad news, however, the official reason has often been restated in terms of performance: "You haven't been producing as well as you used to.")

Many people lose their jobs for chemical reasons. We have found, in fact, that above the $50,000 salary level, 80% of all terminations are caused by poor chemistry. Below this level, by contrast, individual terminations are usually prompted by poor performance. For one thing, performance problems are often easier to pinpoint at junior levels in an organization. Comments like, "He didn't finish the report on time," "She didn't do the project properly," or, "His sales figures dropped three months running," are both easy to quantify and more likely to apply to lower-level employees than to middle and top executives. Individuals at higher levels are more likely to spend their time managing people, an activity that invites problems which result from poor communication.

But poor chemistry can also cause performance problems. If you are a sales manager who says, "We had to let him go because we kept getting bad feedback from our clients about him," you are describing both a chemical and a performance issue. Or, if you are at the other end of the line, and your associates no longer consider you a member of their team, you probably won't be able to deal effectively with them, and you certainly won't be used effectively by them. Your performance inevitably suffers.

Questions of chemistry can create situations that are funny, peculiar, or even irrational and grotesque. For example, we counseled one man who lost an important job because he had very bad breath and body odor. How's that for chemistry? It was also a performance issue: His peers would not get close enough to work with him. No one told him the real reason behind his termination, although it probably wouldn't have helped: It took us a year to get him to change his personal habits. But he was also incredibly competent, and he ultimately landed an excellent new job.

Another man was terminated eight months after his wife made an innocent comment to his boss's wife at a cocktail party. Our client's wife talked about how happy she and her husband had been where they last lived, at his previous job. The boss's wife convinced the boss that the man wasn't happy at his current job. The man loved his work, in fact, and was performing admirably at it. When he was terminated, he was told, "We understand that you weren't happy here, anyway."

"Whatever gave you that idea?" the man asked.

"Oh, a lot of people knew that," he was told.

Individuals often create their own problems. At some point in their careers, for instance, most people discover that they aren't going to become president of the company, that they will not make $250,000 a year, that the long, black automobiles will never come calling for them. This realization can be devastating, particularly for competitive people who have been taught from day one to win. All of a sudden it appears that everyone else is doing better in life: has a better marriage, smarter children, a nicer house, and a brighter future.

One common response to the situation is to blame the job or the company. Superiors rarely understand the situation. "I used to be able to work so well with him," they say, "but lately he's gotten so hostile that I can't even talk to the guy."

Most people work these problems out for themselves. They accept the situation, or they make the move to a more acceptable environment. But others trap themselves in a vicious circle: "I'm not going to make it here," they decide, "but I can't risk trying something else, so I'll stay here." Soon they are added to the list of people who have "turned off" or "burned out" at their jobs, and someone else makes the decision for them.

Some General Steps to Take

These warning signals, reasons for termination, and case histories make the business world seem a very dangerous place. How can anyone's job remain secure in the middle of such uncertainty? The answer is that no job is ever really secure. But the question itself misses the point.

It misses the point because there is no need for jobs to be secure. *People* need to be secure. You don't have to depend on your job if you can depend on yourself.

So what can you do if you see that some of the danger signals strike very close to home? What should you do if one of the reasons for termination seems to have your name written all over it?

First, don't panic.* Congratulate yourself for being realistic and objective about your situation. Realize that many
people simply can't be so honest with themselves. Begin to
consider alternatives and make plans.

The second step is to upgrade your résumé, *not* because
you may be needing it soon, but because the process is a
therapeutic step that helps you begin to take stock of yourself. Writing down the facts of your career forces you to face
them. You may not like a few of them, but we think that you
will be surprised and buoyed by seeing just how much—and
how well—you have actually done in the past. Review your
accomplishments before you proceed.

Next, consider your current job by putting together an
informal job description. Try to decide what is good and bad
about it. Make a list of pros and cons. This will make you
define your job, something you may not have done in years.
You'll see what you should be doing, and, by extension,
you'll learn whether you're actually performing these tasks.

Finally, draw up one additional document. Use an old-
fashioned phrase and call it your "career-path statement."
Write down as much as you can about what you would like
to be doing at this point in your career. Try to decide where
you would like to head. Be specific. Don't shy away from
money you would like to make or where you would be most
happy living.

These three documents let you look at yourself in the
past, the present, and the future. They begin to show you
what your skills are, how well you are using them, and
whether these skills—and your present job—are leading you in
a direction that will reward you tomorrow. Do you perform
well enough to stand behind your work? Are you maintaining
visibility in your field by participating in business organizations or on industry committees? Are you keeping abreast

* If you're reading this book because you just *did* lose your job, you may
decide that the suggestion "Don't panic" belongs in a list called "Things
that are easy for them to say." True. But you *are* reading this book, which
shows that you have started to take deliberate steps to find a new job, and
that is the opposite of panicking.

and staying aware of the direction your business is heading?

This is also a good time to think about taking advantage of professional career guidance resources. Many psychologists specialize in career counseling. Or, you can contact organizations that administer tests which determine skills and aptitudes. Vocational counselors can work with you to determine where you should head with your career. (There are sharks in the water—charlatans skilled in separating you from your money. Before you sign on any dotted line, read chapter six.)

Should You Quit First?

But what if you decide that you have more immediate problems? What if you think that—right here and now—your job is on the line?

You have three general options. First, you can choose to leave your job immediately, either by simply resigning or by negotiating your departure. Second, you can try to save the day by working actively to strengthen your position at work. Third, you can continue to work in much the same way that you have in the past, realizing, however, that you might be terminated and making plans to make the most of the situation if that occurs.

When should you quit? If you can absolutely no longer tolerate your job, if your dissatisfaction is causing performance-related problems that you think might haunt your career in the future, or if unhappiness caused by your job is ruining the rest of your life, then it may be best to walk in to the boss, tell him that things simply aren't working out, and announce your decision to resign.

There are, of course, certain drawbacks connected to this plan of action. Does this company pay severance to people who resign? How will you support yourself while you look for a new job? Will you have enough time to spend on your job search, or will you have to worry about the mortgage and how to convert your company medical coverage to a private plan?

Also, are you certain that the situation is intolerable? Are you *convinced* that you have interpreted your position correctly? Many observers think that the current trend to jump from one job to another is caused in part by a growing reluctance to face problems and solve them. Rather than work out difficulties that come up in their jobs, more and more people choose not to risk failure by simply walking away to another job. The problem here, of course, is that no job comes free of problems, so there is never an end to hopping from one job to the next. What results is a classic example of the job controlling the person rather than the person controlling his future.

Finally, many people—including, perhaps, some potential future employers—are convinced that smart people don't leave one job until they have another to take its place. Who hasn't been told that it's easier to find a job if you have a job?

This may be true, but it is also true that finding the right job is generally a full-time occupation. You stand the best chance of finding the best job when you can apply all your energy to the task.

Suppose you are asked, "Why aren't you working now?" You answer can be, "When I realized that my former job would not take me in the direction I wanted to go, I decided to look elsewhere. I discovered that I couldn't carry on a proper search without neglecting my job. I didn't want to shortchange my boss, so I resigned."

This may work, or it may not. So you owe it to yourself to consider all the risks before deciding to resign. At the very least, make it a rational process. (It goes without saying that the absolute worst thing to do is to get angry one day, insult your boss, and quit. That's not resignation, it's self-destruction.) Even if you have given careful thought to your situation, and even if you have concluded that resigning is the sensible thing to do, think it through once or twice more. Consider the other options that may be available to you. (Remember, the worst they can do is fire you.)

Negotiating Your Way Out of a Job

You might be able to negotiate your way out of your job. There is substantial risk involved, but under the proper conditions, negotiating can bring excellent results. The process involves telling your boss that you have given serious thought to leaving the company, but that you want the move to be as smooth as possible—both for yourself and for him—and discussing whether the two of you can work out a method for doing so. Perhaps he can assign special projects to you so that, free from normal routine, you can spend some of your time concentrating on your job search. You might agree to help select and train the person who will replace you so that the transition is orderly.

The idea makes a great deal of sense because it minimizes trauma and disruption for both the company and you. After all, if you resign immediately, your boss has a problem. He must find a replacement—never an easy task—and until he does, someone else in the organization must add your duties to his own.

But don't underestimate the risks. If you go in to negotiate your way out of a job, you have to be prepared to resign if the process doesn't work. Your boss' response could be, "Well, yes, let's see what we can work out." But it could also be, "If you're telling me that you don't want to work here, then you'd better plan to leave soon." Or it could be, "Well, you've obviously made up your mind to resign, and I think it's best to make it effective immediately." You could easily end up with no severance and no benefits.

When one large corporation terminated a group of executives as part of a major reorganization, one man tried to negotiate his way *into* the group of people who were let go. He was highly regarded by management and they wanted him to stay, but the cutbacks and the general direction that the company seemed to be taking troubled the man, and he wished to leave. He tried to negotiate his own settlement, but it did not turn out well. His superiors worried that if they agreed to his request, they would set a dangerous precedent: Other people in the organization, people they wanted to keep, might be tempted to resign and ask for the same settlement package. They gave the man nothing.

Negotiated resignations and settlements will no doubt become more common in the future, because in many cases they meet the needs of all involved. But there is still enough resistance to the idea—enough of a feeling that it isn't quite right to "reward" people for quitting the company—to make it difficult for many employers to agree to such programs today.

If you sense that the environment in your organization is receptive to this kind of idea, however, if you have good experience and a good track record, and if you have a solid relationship with your boss, it may well be a good idea. You could even be pleasantly surprised. You give the company a chance to suggest alternatives when you bring up the idea of a negotiated settlement, and if they want to, they have the opportunity to make you a counter-offer that you can't refuse. But you must also be willing to accept other consequences, and this may include having to resign.

Strengthening Your Hold

It is more likely that you do not want to leave your job. What if you don't wish to resign? Are there things you can do to strengthen your hold on your current, tenuous position?

If you sense that things are going badly, talk with your boss. Ask if there are steps you can take to do your job better. But make sure that you're not looking to be stroked, coddled, and complimented. Make certain that you are really looking for suggestions and that you are willing to listen to them. If your boss says, "Well, as a matter of fact, you're not doing very well at all," and your response is, "How can you say that?" you aren't likely to improve matters.

You might even force the issue. If you ask, "How am I doing?" you give your boss the opportunity to think, "Oh, why wait any longer? I might as well get this unpleasant business over with right now." (If that should occur, you can console yourself with the knowledge that nothing was likely to have reversed the course of events. At least you took an active hand in the process.)

The principal difficulty with trying to work out these problems on your own is that they are often based on "chemistry" issues. If you have trouble communicating with your boss, or if he has difficulty communicating with you, chances are slim that the two of you will be able to talk your problems away.

During the past few years, our firm has created and refined a management service called Directional Counseling, a program that helps companies work with problem performers to avoid having to terminate them. In the process, a trained counselor works both with the employee who is not performing well and with the individual's boss. Two important characteristics make this process different from an individual's attempts to correct a difficult situation on his or her own.

First, both the boss and the employee are committed to solving the problem. The boss, by investing his time and his company's money, has agreed to participate in the project. The individual takes the program seriously because he has been told, in no uncertain terms, that his or her job is in jeopardy. Second, the counselor keeps the process on track. When the participants fall into the kind of behavior patterns that caused the problem in the first place, the counselor helps them resolve issues rather than magnify them.

So it may be unrealistic to expect too great a response from personal attempts to salvage your job. This is where the third option makes sense. Continue to do your job. Try to perform as well as you can, so that you can stand behind your work. At the same time, arm yourself so that if you do lose your job, you'll be prepared to move to a new and more rewarding position. To do this, you'll need to learn the art of getting fired.

2 * The Art of Getting Fired

No ONE ever taught you how to get fired. You probably haven't had much in the way of practical experience about losing your job. What happens? How will you react? And most important, how *should* you respond to being terminated?

If this were a perfect world, losing a job would be a straightforward matter. Your boss would call you into his office one morning early in the week. He'd get right to the point: "I have bad news. I'm going to have to let you go."

He would give concrete reasons for the decision: "In the past six months, you've been seriously late with three reports. We discussed these problems at least once a week during that period, and I suggested a number of things you might do to improve your performance. Last week, you were late with another project. When you did turn it in, the work wasn't satisfactory. The task had to be reassigned to another member of the department. Now we're seriously behind in our group objectives, and I've decided that I have to make a change immediately."

He'd take no more than five minutes to describe the chain of events that prompted your termination. Then he would listen. He'd try to get you to talk and would keep trying until he was convinced that you understood his decision and your position. He wouldn't argue with you, or apologize, or make promises he couldn't keep, or attack you personally. He wouldn't try to get you to agree with his decision but would simply want you to accept it as a fact.

Then he would talk about your severance package. He'd tell how much severance you would receive and how it would be distributed—in regular installments so that your benefits would continue intact. He would describe how your other company benefits would be affected: medical coverage and life insurance policies, for example, as well as profit-sharing, pension plans, and other perks and fringe benefits.

He might tell you that office space and secretarial help had been reserved for you for a specific length of time to help you make the move to a new job. He might say that the company would supply outplacement counseling during your job search. He'd probably give you a letter describing all the details of the support package he had just described.

Finally, he would identify your next step. He might introduce you to an outplacement specialist. He'd at least tell you where to go when you left his office and who to contact at the company if, later, you had additional questions. He would finish by suggesting that you take time to think about and plan your future before making any immediate decisions.

The meeting would be businesslike, and the conversation would avoid pontification and recrimination.

If this were an ideal world, here's what your reaction might be. "I obviously don't agree with your decision," you might say, "but it's pretty clear that my immediate concerns have to revolve around my next job and the things I need to get to it.

"I feel that I'll need six months' severance as a bridge to new employment," you would continue. "I also think that my fringe benefits—including my company car—should be continued during that period. I'll have more important things to do than worry about transportation. I'd like to receive outplacement counseling. After all, I've spent my time working at this job, not trying to find another one, and I admit that I'm out of practice when it comes to searching for work.

"This is obviously a shock and a surprise to me," you would add. "You've had time to think about the situation. I haven't. Right now, I need to think. I'd like to meet with you tomorrow to discuss reference statements, my profit-sharing benefits, and anything else that needs to be resolved."

And then you'd leave.

This isn't a perfect world, however, and neither you nor your boss is likely to act quite so coolly or rationally.

If you've never received lessons in getting fired, he was probably never taught how to fire anyone. Unless he's a whip-toting sadist (in which case you should dance through the halls giving thanks for being rid of him), he won't enjoy the task. No matter how justified he may feel, he's likely to be uneasy or even frightened. (We have witnessed situations in which the person doing the termination was more distraught than the individual who was being fired.) No one likes to make enemies, and firing people has never been a surefire way to make friends.

Your boss may delay the confrontation for days or even weeks. As time passes, his anxiety will grow. When he does call you into his office, he may combat this uneasiness by moving toward either of two extremes.

He may decide that the best defense is a good offense. The result can be an insensitive, even brutal, termination. Real and imagined sins may be dragged up. Your boss may try to turn his decision into a group effort: "No one can get along with you," he might say, or, "Your people don't support you anymore." He may try to wring a confession of guilt or admission of failure from you. "You agree that you've done a poor job, don't you?" he may ask, or, "You can see that I have no alternative, right?" or, "You never did like it here, did you?"

There probably won't be much of a discussion, and you may never discover the real reasons for your termination.

Your boss is unsure of himself and terribly ill at ease. He needs to convince himself that he's made the right decision, and overkill seems his best strategy.

On the other hand, your boss might wander off in the opposite direction and never get to the point. He may tell himself that he's worried about how you will react to the bad news, and convince himself that he's trying to soften the blow, although he's really trying to make things easy on himself. In this case, you will find yourself in for a particularly surreal conversation.

You'll drink coffee, discuss the weather, and talk about your families. Finally your boss will say, "Well, I don't know how to. . . . How *have* things been going lately?" You'll begin to deliver a progress report, and your boss will make lame attempts to bring the conversation around to the subject of termination . . . your termination.

He may not succeed, and you may walk out of his office in a state of limbo. "I'm not sure we can continue this way," he may say. "You'd better go talk to Personnel. Maybe we can find you a job somewhere else in the company." You leave wondering what has happened, and he sits hoping that someone in Personnel will tell you the *real* news. You have been fired, but no one has delivered the message. You're in corporate never-never land.

Your boss could even head in both misguided directions, circling the issue awkwardly at first, growing frantic when he discovers that things aren't progressing like a business school case study, over-reacting and then lumbering in for a messy kill. If you are able to remain calm and objective in the midst of such a barrage, you might turn this lack of control to your own advantage and negotiate an exceptionally comfortable severance package for yourself.

But you probably won't. Even if your boss is calm, supportive, and on top of the situation, you may not be. As soon as you realize that you have lost your job, you may be besieged by uncomfortable feelings and emotions. And when the termination interview is finished, your boss gets to go back to his normal life. You don't. You've just been shoved into what appears to be a very uncertain new world.

Five Reactions to Termination

The bottom line tends to be a firm conviction that you have lost control of your life. You feel that you ceased to be in charge of things the moment your job was taken from you. You have lost the structure it provided, and the habits and rules that shaped your life an hour ago do not seem to fit this new and abnormal situation.

You are likely to react in one of five ways. You may be violent or you may be euphoric. You may react by trying to escape or you may respond with total disbelief. Or you may have anticipated the termination and react accordingly. Let's look at this last reaction first.

Anticipation.   This is the most typical reaction to termination. It is likely to occur to anyone who has thought—rightly or not—that he or she might lose a job. If, for instance, you decided that one or more of the danger signs we discussed previously applied to your situation, and you subsequently lost your job, you'd be likely to have an "anticipated" reaction.

You may be surprised and shocked by your termination, but the shock results from having your worst fears confirmed, not from being totally surprised by the decision. You may never have acted on these fears, and you may never even have admitted them openly to yourself. But at one level or another, you recognized them.

When the actual termination does occur, you're somewhat prepared for it. Your reaction is not likely to be too intense. You may say, "I don't think that this is all my fault," or, "It's too bad we couldn't work together," but you're likely to realize what the situation is and accept it as a real, if unpleasant, fact of life.

Some people anticipate termination to such a degree

that they try to escape it before it ever occurs: They avoid their bosses, don't return telephone calls, even stay away from their offices for days at a time.

When they do get fired, they may be relieved. The pressure is off, and they don't have to hide any longer.

Other people are angry, or scared, or ashamed. But their feelings are not so intense that they become paralyzed. The common denominator to this reaction is the relative ease with which the individual accepts his or her fate.

The termination interview is not likely to be extremely emotional, as a result, and the individual is able to concentrate on practical matters related to the severance package and to the future.

Disbelief.   You may not anticipate your termination at all, and your reaction may be complete disbelief. You'll feel totally shocked, and you'll say things like, "You can't do this to me," or, "I won't allow this," or, "This simply can't be happening to me." You may plead to keep your job, or you may beg for another position somewhere else in the company. You probably won't let yourself be drawn into a real conversation and will answer questions with a simple "yes" or "no." Or you may not accept the situation at all. You might tell your boss that you really ought to get back to work. You've decided to react by not reacting at all.

This can be a dangerous reaction to losing a job. We worked with one client who had been employed by the same company for 20 years. He rose through the ranks to become a plant manager, knew how to run every piece of equipment on the premises, but never learned how to delegate.

The pager he wore on his belt alerted him to the slightest problem even if he was 50 miles from the plant; he was on call twenty-four hours a day. His subordinates had standing orders to beep him when *anything* happened.

He ran his plant for eight years in this fashion, until the strain began to show. Serious problems developed at the manufacturing facility.

On a Friday afternoon, the company fired him and put

him on a plane to Chicago for outplacement counseling. We had assumed that he wouldn't come until Monday morning, and when he didn't arrive at our office, we called his former employer and learned that he'd been on his own all weekend. We called his hotel and got no answer at his room. When we went to his room and knocked on the door, the only response was a slight moan. A bell captain let us in.

He was sitting in a chair, his feet drawn up to his chest in a fetal position. He shook uncontrollably. He hadn't shaved or showered. He thought he was going to die. He had never figured out what had hit him.

He was a capable and talented man, but it took six months of intensive counseling before he felt confident enough to go to an interview. He started a new career, became a first-line supervisor and within two years was back in charge of a large organization.

Escape. You can also react to being terminated by trying to escape the situation. "I can't stand this," you tell yourself, "I'm getting out of here." You understand what has happened to you, but you don't know what to do and decide that flight is the best option.

You may leave the termination interview before you understand the terms of your support package and go home to announce that you'll have to sell the house when, in fact, the company intends to continue your regular salary for six months or a year. You may head for the nearest tavern where, well-fortified, you share your troubles with a less-than-adoring public. People have even skipped out of termination interviews and called newspaper reporters—sharing their problems in the most public and potentially self-destructive manner imaginable.

Euphoria. You might react as if you are delighted to hear the news that you have been fired. You tell your boss that you are positive that you can handle the situation. Your boss is overjoyed; you've made a sticky chore easy.

That may present a problem. Euphoric reactions occur to people who are so highly geared to taking directions from their bosses that they agree to be terminated just as they would agree to work overtime.

If you think that you've gotten where you are in life by agreeing to everything, why stop now? Keep agreeing, and the boss will take care of you. The trouble with this approach is that you really don't understand exactly where you've gotten in life.

We counseled one woman who seemed positively overjoyed about her situation. She was excited, outgoing, and an absolute pleasure to work with. It took her two-and-a-half years to find a new job. It took us that long to get her to be realistic about her situation without losing her enthusiasm. Nothing that was offered to her seemed "real," she said, and when she talked to potential employers, she left an impression that she wasn't seriously looking for a job.

Violence. The reaction that terminators and terminees fear most is the violent response: "What if I punch him in the mouth?" an employee wonders halfway through a termination interview. "What if he punches me in the mouth?" his boss asks himself. It is actually the least common response to the situation. Almost everyone feels some degree of anger at being terminated, but most people control these emotions; even those who do make threats are less likely to carry them out than to feel sheepish about having made them.

If there is violence during a termination, it is usually verbal. You may scream, holler obscenities, suggest that you will sue the company, or indicate that you will pull it down with you by publicizing damaging news.

Not long ago, we decided that we would have to terminate one of our own employees. (It happens everywhere.) We sat down in his office with him and launched what we thought would be a brilliant termination interview. When he heard the news, he shouted at us for a minute, jumped from his chair, threw open the door of his office, and began yelling at his secretary, telling her it was all her fault and condemning her for not supporting him.

Not having the faintest idea what was going on, she

burst into tears. He stormed off to the receptionist, started in on her, and barged out of the office.

Later, he tried to make amends. Still later, he asked his former secretary to help him with some typing as he began his job search. "Not on your life," she said.

Five Common Emotions

When you react violently to losing your job, you are venting the anger that the situation has created. There are other feelings and emotions that are commonly associated with termination. The people that we counsel tell us that one, or several, or frequently all of the following emotions surfaced almost immediately after they learned that they had lost their jobs.

Anger. Someone has just taken something very valuable from you—your job—and you feel furious. Who do they think they are? How can the company let your boss cover his failures by taking *your* job? You have spent years working for them, and this is what you get in return.

Shame. You have lost something valuable, and you have an unpleasant feeling that it's your own fault. How could you do this to yourself? How could you be so dumb that you never saw it coming and never did anything to avoid it? How will you ever face your family and friends? How could you be such a failure?

Fear. A central part of your life's structure has been taken away suddenly, and you don't know what the consequences will be. How will you pay the mortgage? What about your children's tuition bills? Is this going to ruin your marriage? Are your friends going to ridicule you? What will this do to your career? Will you ever find another job?

Sadness. You have lost your job, and that is cause for mourning. You'll never find another to match it. Life will never be this good again. It's all downhill from here. This is the end of the world.

Self-pity. You don't deserve this fate. How could *they* do *this* to *you?* Why, of all people, were you singled out? Why not somebody else? You just did your job, stayed out of politics, and look at the thanks you got.

These are the most common emotions, but they aren't the only possibilities. We have mentioned, for instance, that some people feel relieved when they lose their jobs. If you have been hanging on to a really unpleasant position, and if the pressure has been eating you alive, then you have every right to feel relieved if you get fired. As a matter of fact, you have every right to feel *any* emotion, no matter how ugly it may seem. The question is: What do you do with these feelings?

The Art of Getting Fired

What can you do to improve the situation, or does the art of getting fired refer to rolling up your own sleeves to help your boss slit your wrists?

There is most definitely something to do, and the key to the process is realizing that, while you cannot control how you feel, you can control how you act. The art of losing a job involves taking control of a very negative incident and turning it into a positive situation. You can accomplish this by identifying all of your options and measuring each against a single yardstick: What is the best thing you can do for yourself in this situation?

Imagine you are in a termination interview and have just heard the words, "We're going to have to let you go." Pretend that you can stop the world for a half-hour to discuss your options with a trusted advisor.

"Well, how do you feel?" he asks.

"I'm angry," you answer. "How could they do that to me? I'm going to let that guy know just how angry I really am. I'll blister his ears."

"That's definitely an option," your advisor says, "but

what's it going to do for you? Do you really think that he
doesn't know you're angry? Will telling him off get you a
better reference when you need one?"

"But I'm really angry," you say. "That guy didn't look
out for me, he's a liar, he's dead wrong. I'm going to be
manly (or womanly) and punch him in the mouth (or kick
him somewhere else)."

"That's certainly an option," your confidant says, "and
it might make you feel better, but it might also land you in
jail. How will that help?"

"But I'm angry," you say.

"And you have every right to be angry," your friend answers. "But if you hand him that anger now, all you'll do is
convince him that he made the right decision. He'll say
you're acting like a child, and deserve to get spanked. So let's
assume that's an inappropriate choice.

"Now," your advisor continues, "what else do you feel?"

"I feel really sorry for myself. I didn't deserve this."

"What can you do about it?"

"I can go over my boss's head and beg *his* boss to give
me my job back."

"That's an option," your friend says, "but what's it
going to get you? Isn't it likely that your boss already cleared
this with his boss? Didn't the personnel department, and the
legal department, and who knows what other departments,
sign off on this decision, too? What have you got to gain by
trying to hang on by your fingernails? How are you going to
get the best possible deal for yourself by taking this route?"

You can consider all your options in this way. If you feel
ashamed of the situation, you may conclude that running
from the room and out of the building is a pretty good idea.
Ask how that will help you. If you're not letting yourself feel
any emotions yet, you may be pretending that it's all a bad
dream and that nothing's really happened. Will that view
improve matters?

This process should begin to warn you away from useless
or self-destructive paths of action. But what if you simply

cannot control your emotions. What if you think that, whether or not it's a good idea, you're about to be really angry? What if you're getting ready to cry?

The best thing to do is leave. But don't run away, and don't try to convince yourself that nothing is wrong. Tell your boss that his decision has taken you completely by surprise. Say that you need time to think about the situation. Tell him (and remind yourself) that this is a critical issue for you, and say that you need time to consider your options so that you can deal sensibly with them. Make an appointment to see him the following day. (Don't wait much longer than that. As time passes, the company loses interest in you and may become more difficult to deal with.)

Unless you feel very sure of yourself, postponing matters for a day makes good sense. You'll have some time to come to terms with your emotions, and you'll be less likely to do or say something that could return to haunt you when you look for a new job. You're dealing with an important life issue; you ought to have your wits about you.

If you decide to leave immediately, do just that: Leave immediately. Don't go back to your office. Don't start a conversation with anyone. If someone comes up and says, "You don't look too good. Is everything o.k.?" answer that something has come up, you have to leave immediately, and you'll tell them about it in the morning. Go home. Avoid liquor. Don't telephone everyone you've ever known. Don't try to contact the president of the company.

If you feel that you may really lose control of yourself by doing something that will hurt you or someone around you, get professional help immediately. Call your doctor or contact a psychologist or psychiatrist. (We mention this sort of crisis as a possibility. We are sensitive to it and watch out for it in our business. It's not a situation to fool with, so if you're not sure of yourself, get a professional's opinion.)

What if you are in good enough control of both the

situation and yourself to continue the dialogue with your former employer immediately?*

What you need to take home with you is an understanding of what the company is prepared to do for you. They have undoubtedly figured out the severance package already, and you need to know the details. How much will you be given and how will it be paid to you? (In the next chapter you'll learn why regular checks are preferable to a single large payment.)

What will happen to your fringe benefits? Will your medical coverage continue as long as you receive severance pay? What about profit-sharing and your company's pension plan? What will become of your other fringe benefits—a life insurance policy, for example, or a company car or club membership?

Will the company provide additional support as you look for a new job? Will they give you an office, will they answer your phone calls, will they provide secretarial support? Will they pay for outplacement counseling to help you sharpen your job-search skills?

Beyond these practical considerations, you'll also want to learn—as accurately as you can—exactly what caused your termination. You need to know precisely what happened, not because you might save your job (you're over that thought by now), but because the information will help you plan for the future. It may not be pleasant: You may be told that you drink too much, or that you never meet deadlines, or that your department really *did* think you were an animal. But you should ask the question nevertheless.

Be aware, however, that you may not get a straight answer, particularly if you are being fired for reasons connected to personal chemistry. In addition, the company's legal staff may have told your boss what to say and what not to say.

If you don't agree with something in the severance pack-

* If you nodded agreement as you read the word "former," give yourself a gold star. You're beginning to realize that you no longer work for this company. Now you work for yourself.

age, or if you're not sure whether you should agree with one or more of its clauses, the best thing to do is to say, "I'm not sure about that, but I want to take some time to put my thoughts in order. Can we get together tomorrow to finish up?"

If your boss replies, "I'm sorry, but that's all there is, and that's all there's going to be," you should say, "I understand that we're at an impasse, but I really need more time to think, so it would be best if we met tomorrow." Don't say, "Well, that's o.k.," to something that isn't. But don't be argumentative, and don't be defensive. Make the best of the situation.

Realize that the period from the time the company tells you that you've been terminated to the time you leave the office for good is an extremely delicate interval. It may last ten minutes, or ten minutes plus the next day, or perhaps for a much longer period of time. As long as you're there, measure everything you do against its potential effect on your future. How will it influence the search for your next job?

When you do leave for the day, go home. You have a busy seventy-two hours ahead of you.

3 * The First Seventy-two Hours

$\mathbf{D}$ON'T get mad, get even" is a popular saying and, if you've just lost your job, a silly piece of advice. You deserve better counsel:

Get mad, but don't get even; *get ahead.*

You have two immediate priorities: dealing with your emotions (getting mad) and answering several practical, or "survival," questions. Tackling these issues helps you orient yourself away from the past (and the urge to get even) and toward the future (and the opportunity to get ahead). During the first seventy-two hours after you have been terminated, you should concentrate on understanding and accepting what happened to you so that you can begin to devote your energies to the practical business of finding a new job. What you do and how you react during this three-day period will determine the general ease or difficulty with which you will find new employment in the weeks and months ahead.

This is easier said than done, of course. Major concerns surface just when you feel most vulnerable. Being "on the street" is no longer a cliché but a new and unpleasant fact of your life. Your emotions threaten to engulf you: Confronting them may seem particularly risky just now. You've been handed a difficult assignment—finding a new job. You haven't asked for it, you probably don't know how to proceed, and all of a sudden you feel very much alone.

You may be convinced that you, and your life, are suddenly and totally out of control. To top it off, here are two men with comfortable jobs (as of this writing, anyway) telling you to take control of stormy emotions and niggling details.

Our first piece of advice sounds simple, but it probably won't be: Do nothing. Your immediate impulse is likely to be: "I need a job, any job, and I need it right now." This is the vocational equivalent of remounting the horse that just threw you. But with horses (as with job finding), you can save yourself a great deal of pain by assessing the damage, figuring out why you got thrown, and adapting your plans accordingly before climbing back aboard.

Resist the temptation to call business associates or to contact search firms. You're not ready to talk to either. Getting a new job is a systematic process, and if you do things out of sequence, you penalize yourself. Don't talk to people now about getting a replacement job. You don't know what to say to them yet, and you'll probably scare them off. Later, when they can really help you, you may not be able to call on them if you've spooked them this early in the game.

Dealing with Emotions

The important thing is to start the process and to stick with it. Look at your emotions first.

In the previous chapter, we discussed the need to control your feelings during your termination interview, no matter how greatly you may have wanted to scream or moan or strangle your former boss. Once you leave the building, however, what's best for you changes. Now you need to vent your emotions, to get them out of your gut and into the open in a way that is safe for you and for the people who are important to you.

What happens if you don't? If you hang on to your emotions, they'll trip you up later in the job search process.

In a job interview two months from now (if you get that far), you'll be asked a question about your former employer. Let your bottled-up anger show, and a prospective new boss may wonder whether you might use the same language to describe him at some future time. Utter as tame a phrase as, "I never could get along with those people," and your words may be transmitted up and down the pipeline in slightly different fashion: "He has trouble getting along with people." Try to hide your anger, and you'll furrow your brow, clench your teeth, and hiss something about the "fine company" you used to work for. You won't fool anyone, and you may earn a reputation for perpetual bitterness.

We are acquainted with one employer who will not hire anyone who says anything negative—however mild—about a former employer. He might be looking to hire a great engineer, and he might be convinced that you are a great engineer, but if he hears you say, "Gee, they didn't treat me too well at my last job," he simply won't consider you for the position.

Don't imagine that you can hide your emotions. If you've just lost a job, the fact is written all over your face. Two groups of people normally sit in the reception area of our New York headquarters: representatives of companies interested in our services, and recently terminated individuals who are beginning the outplacement counseling process. To our knowledge, no one has ever confused a member of one group with a member of the other. Losing a job is a powerful emotional shock, and it shows.

Don't think that your emotions will go away if you simply ignore them. If you don't do something with them, they'll grow. Refuse to deal with your feelings of self-pity, anger, and failure, and a potential employer may conclude: "He left that job six months ago, and he still hasn't gotten over it. He doesn't sound very flexible or adaptable." Continue to feel ashamed about having been fired, and you'll never appear self-assured or self-confident as you look for employment.

We meet most of our clients moments after they have been terminated, so that they can begin to discuss their feelings immediately. When they go home at the end of that first difficult day, they have begun the venting process which helps them identify and accept their emotions.

There are times, however, when we don't begin to work with people until weeks or even months after their terminations. Most have been unsuccessful in their job searches because they have neglected their feelings. They have become rigid and self-destructive, and have been running in circles (or staring off into space) rather than finding new jobs. Putting them in touch with these feelings, a task that might once have taken three days, may now take three weeks or even three months.

Our advice about dealing with your emotions is simple: The longer you wait, the harder it gets, so do something now. Talk to someone. Tell him or her how you feel, what you think and where it hurts. You need a friendly, supportive, non-competitive shoulder to lean on.

If you are married, your husband or wife is your most obvious choice, but not the only person—and perhaps not even the best individual—to turn to. Your spouse could feel more threatened by the loss of your job than you do, and he or she might not be able to provide the calm, understanding assistance that you need. In addition, there is often a correlation between trouble at work and trouble at home. Losing a job is not likely to strengthen a weak marriage, and if your relationship is troubled, your spouse may not be able to give much support, and you may not be willing to accept it.

If you decide to call on someone other than your husband or wife for emotional support, however, don't pretend that you can keep your termination a secret from your family. You may feel scared and ashamed, and you may be tempted to suffer alone. You could even leave home at the normal time each morning, your pockets stuffed with dimes and your destination a telephone booth from which you plan to conduct a secret job search. That has actually happened and, to our knowledge, has only increased the trauma of the job search. The idea of a secret job search is a contradiction in terms.

But suppose it does work. You find a wonderful new job to replace the one you lost (and neglected to mention). You rush home to tell your spouse the good news, and he or she is furious—and rightly so—at being cut out of your life at a critical moment. Your next search could be for a new family.

Losing your job doesn't have to ruin your marriage, of course. It can even improve the situation if your spouse is willing and able to provide help and you can accept it. Couples frequently tell us that they pulled together for the first time in years when one partner had to find a new job suddenly.

What other person might you turn to? A close friend often makes a good confidant. People frequently ask members of the clergy for help; even if a priest or minister has no training as a job counselor, he is likely to be supportive. You could get in touch with a professional vocational counselor, or a psychologist or psychiatrist. Don't think that you are weak to seek help. It's a sign of strength and an indication that you want to improve your situation and not wallow in it.

Professional credentials, incidentally, can indicate experience or expertise, but they may not be necessary. Your most important consideration should be to find someone who is willing to listen to you, to draw you out, and to support you. You need someone who won't make judgments about how you feel but will encourage you to blow off steam. He or she should simply be able to keep you talking so that you can air your feelings in a safe environment.

Professional counselors use a number of tactics to help people vent their emotions. They ask open-ended questions, for instance, to encourage wide-ranging answers rather than "yes" or "no" replies. As a simple example, instead of saying, "Do you feel sad?" the answer to which is likely to be, "Yes," they might ask, "How sad do you feel?" which prompts an answer like, "I'm so sad that . . ."

They use restatement and reflection to draw people out. If you say, "I just got fired," they say, "You mean they let you go after all these years?" If you say, "I feel terrible," they might ask, "Well, what does that make you want to do?"

If you're having trouble talking about your feelings, they'll ask questions to get you started: "What's the one thing that is uppermost in your mind right now?" they might ask, or, "What do you think your first step should be?"

The questions are simple enough, and they involve no psychological mumbo-jumbo. Trained outplacement counselors have a body of experience and knowledge to draw on—they've done this many times before—and that makes them adept at keeping the venting process on track. But a good listener's most important attributes are compassion and understanding, traits that are rarely the result of training.

There are, on the other hand, counterproductive traits to watch out for in would-be confidants, patterns that trained counselors are not likely to exhibit if they work with a reputable organization. Look out, for example, for people who speak in clichés.

Someone tells you, "I know just how you feel." (Oh, no, he doesn't.) He says, "It's not all that bad." (How on earth does he know how bad it is? It certainly feels "that bad.") He tells you, "No problem, you'll find a job easily." (How can he be so sure?)

Be especially alert for people who make judgments about your situation. "Gee, how the devil did you get yourself in this mess?" they may ask. "Don't you think you should have seen it coming?" Even if you *should* have seen it coming, you don't need to be reminded of that fact now. Some people—even close friends—cannot refrain from attacking other people—particularly close friends—regardless of the circumstances. Say, "Thanks for the help," and find someone else to talk to.

Now is not the time for advice, so be wary of anyone who offers you a list of immediate suggestions: "O.K., now the first thing you ought to do is call Frank Jones at Acme, then you should see . . ." The purpose of the venting process is to finish dealing with the past in order to prepare yourself for dealing with the future. Don't let someone put the cart before the horse for you. Find a person who is comfortable saying nothing more than, "I'm here, what's on your mind?"

Your role in the venting process is to say whatever *is* on your mind and to work to bring your feelings and emotions into the open. If you feel angry, describe how you feel angry. If you feel stupid for letting all this happen to you, try to say why. If you think it's all your former boss' fault, here is the right time and the safe place to say so. If you blame your wife because she wouldn't move to Cleveland, talk about it (but not, perhaps, to your wife just yet). If you think that you are a failure because you never went to graduate school, get that off your chest. If the whole mess is a conspiracy, mention that, too.

Don't be sensible. The purpose of this process is not to make sense but to clear the air. You're doing fine if you find yourself saying, "This may sound crazy, but . . . ," or "This is totally illogical, but I feel . . ."

The more feelings that surface the better. In fact, you should be most concerned if you don't feel anything but sit paralyzed in a sea of failure and rejection. Don't let yourself get mired in this sort of silent self-pity. Talk about it.

How long should the venting process continue? In one sense it never really ends, because you never quite get over being fired. Five years from now, when you are happily and successfully working somewhere else, something may remind you of the day you lost your job. "That still makes me furious," you may think. "I'll never understand how I let that happen," you may tell yourself. The difference, of course, will be that you'll spend a few moments lost in thought, then shake your head and go back to work.

Right now the situation seems a good deal more pressing and threatening. But at some point in the venting process, you will see a change in your reactions. It may take three hours, two days, or five days. But sooner or later you will notice that your thoughts are beginning to shift: from what has happened to what to do next. One moment you are complaining about the raw deal you got, and the next minute you may say, "Well, that's enough of that. What am I going to do now?" This is a signal that the healing process has begun and that you are ready to start dealing with other needs.

Three days of venting is a good target to aim for. By the end of that time, you will probably have exhausted and digested your emotions so that you can live with them. If it only takes a day to reach that point, so much the better. If the process lasts for four or five days, that's fine, too. If you're still at it after much more than a week, however, it's time to take a good look at the situation.

You may simply be procrastinating. If the future looks particularly threatening, you may have decided to maintain the status quo for as long as possible. You don't feel too good right now, but, who knows, things could get even worse. Why find out? (The most popular occasion for postponing matters comes later, however, when the time comes to actually talk to someone about employment. Some people spend weeks working on a two-page résumé, telling themselves that it needs to be perfect. What they are actually doing is postponing the day when they have to put themselves on the line by calling or meeting someone about a job.)

You may find that rather than confronting them, you are hoarding or burying your emotions, becoming more bitter and less sure of yourself every day. If this happens, find a professional counselor or psychologist to help get you off dead center and headed in a constructive direction. The process of locating a job is punctuated by ups and downs; if you get stuck anywhere along the way, find someone who can help you get moving again.

At the same time, if you feel that you are ready to move on to other matters, don't conclude that you've seen the last of your emotions, and don't consider it a disaster if unpleasant feelings surface again in the future. They'll just be more of the normal ups and downs, and you'll be able to deal with them, just as you have now.

There is nothing neat or orderly about the search for a good, new job. For the sake of clarity, we have tried to make this discussion move logically from one step to the next, and we have suggested that you simplify the process by trying your best to stick to a plan. Life isn't always quite so predictable, however. We can all be tripped up by it.

We suggested, for instance, that you take no action until you deal with your emotions, a process that may take three days or more. We also suggested that if you did not discuss your severance package during your termination interview, you should schedule a second meeting as quickly as possible, perhaps for the next day. We obviously owe you another suggestion: How do you follow both bits of advice?

You must be your own judge. If you don't feel that you can control your emotions, don't meet with your former employer until you think that you can. The longer you wait, the less interested he may be in your demands. But starting a fist fight or dissolving into tears is likely to help your cause even less. If, on the other hand, you need answers to questions and are reasonably certain that you can conduct the meeting in a temperate, rational manner, go ahead and schedule it, even if you haven't entirely finished the venting process. Consider your options and do what you think will be best for you.

Practical Considerations

When you do shift from emotional matters to practical concerns, your first questions are likely to revolve around one topic: money. How much severance should you receive? How much *will* you get? How will it be disbursed?

As you look for answers to these questions, think of the severance package as a bridge to a new job. Don't look at it as a way to get back at the company or to even the score with your former employer. That approach eats up time, energy, and—if you alienate enough people—perhaps money as well.

It may help matters to think of yourself as a new business. You are the product, and your goal is to sell yourself to a new employer. To do this profitably, you'll need to identify your costs, set objectives, and determine the services that you can provide. You'll have to develop a sales or marketing plan, and eventually, you'll need to put that plan into action.

To start this new business, you need to consider your financing: the severance package. In one sense, you're being given a remarkable opportunity: Your former employer is paying you to work for yourself. You should appreciate that fact; you should also make sure that you get the best possible deal for yourself. Neither consideration can be addressed by concentrating on getting revenge on your old company.

How much severance should you receive?   When we counsel corporations on their severance policies, we recommend that companies support their former employees up to the normal time it would take someone at a comparable employment level to land a new job. We find that, on the average, our clients need five months to make the move to a new position that is right for them.

But we don't suggest that everyone get five months' severance. For one thing, an individual's job level has a significant impact on the length of time he or she needs to find employment. If you earn less than $50,000 a year, for example, our experience indicates that you will need from three to five months to find a new job. If your salary is between $50,000 and $100,000, the process may take from six to eight months. If you are above the $100,000 salary level, you should plan for a job search that may last as long as a year.

The higher you move in a competitive environment, the fewer jobs there are and the longer it is likely to take to find a position that suits your needs and abilities. If you are an experienced chief executive officer from a major corporation, for instance, you are loaded down with qualifications, but there are probably few slots open at any given time that call for your considerable abilities.

The circumstances surrounding a termination can also

affect the conditions of a fair severance package. Suppose, for example, that a company hires an executive away from another firm. In four or five months, management realizes that the decision was a poor one and that the relationship is not working. Given a standard severance policy, the terminated executive would receive a meager separation package. But no one is likely to consider that a fair solution, since the company made at least as big a mistake in offering the job as the individual did in accepting it. The high-level manager now has to start a lengthy job search, and he isn't prepared for it, since the company lured him away from his former employer. Common sense indicates that he needs and deserves a more generous package than any standard formula would be likely to provide.

We recall a situation in which a large industrial company decided that it needed to bring a fresh outlook to its marketing efforts. The company hired a senior marketing manager whose background was in consumer sales, thinking that he might provide the innovative approach sought by the firm. Six months later, everyone realized that their good idea had turned out to be a bad decision, and not because the man wasn't trying: He was doing everything imaginable to make a go of the situation. But members of the company's field sales staff weren't accepting the changes, and neither were the firm's customers.

The idea didn't work, and the executive didn't deserve to be blamed or penalized. The company gave him a severance package that enabled him to concentrate on finding his next job, not on his dwindling bank account.

That should be your goal, too: to get a package that allows you to be concerned with finding a new job, not with making ends meet.

How much severance will you receive?   It is rare to find two companies that share precisely the same severance formula, although the following components, to one degree or another, usually enter into the decision: age of the individual, position within the firm, salary, and length of service. Different companies give different weight to each variable. Age may be more important than salary to one employer, while at another company, length of service may carry more weight than position within the firm.

At least one large, well-known corporation gives a flat, six-week termination payment to everyone, regardless of an individual's age, rank, or serial number. Other companies offer a full year's severance to people who have been with them for less than five years.

So the first thing you should do is determine whether your former employer has a formal severance policy, so that you can at least make certain that you fare as well as anyone else at your level. This will be your bottom line, but it doesn't necessarily have to end up being the package you receive. Suppose you conclude, for instance, that it will take six months to find the right job, and your company offers you four months' severance. Is there anything you can do?

You can try to negotiate an open-ended severance agreement. Consult your former boss. Assure him that you are planning—and are determined to carry out—a serious, full-time employment campaign, but that you may need more time to find a good job than the company's payment plan provides for. Try to get him to agree that if you haven't found work by the end of the formal support period, but have worked hard at the process all along, the company will continue your severance payments for a month or two more. The only real chance you have of securing such an agreement is to convince your former employer that you will devote all your energies to finding a new job. Offer to supply regular progress reports as you carry on your search, so that you can demonstrate how seriously you take the task.

If the company will not accept your proposal for an open-ended agreement—and many will not for fear of setting a dangerous precedent—you may be able to arrange an informal agreement with your former boss. When your severance period elapses, it is likely that he will have to take some action to have you removed from the payroll. If he chooses to, he may be able to delay the process for several weeks or a month, perhaps by as simple a maneuver as not getting around to completing the necessary paperwork for that length of time. Your personal relationship with him will obviously influence his willingness to do so—a good argument for the importance of acting calmly throughout the termination process. He is unlikely to go out of his way to help you if, on the day that he fired you, you called him a lout and a gorilla.

But even if your boss does agree to such a plan, remember that the situation could change drastically before it is ever put into effect. He might be promoted, transferred, or even terminated before your severance period ends and as a result, not be able to help. Or, four or six months from now, he may no longer *want* to assist you.

If you decide to seek either a formal or informal agreement to extend your severance period, you need to act quickly. Your former boss is likely to remain somewhat concerned about your future immediately after your termination. Four or five months later, he probably won't want to be reminded of the incident.

How should your severance be disbursed?   With only a few specific exceptions, we advise our clients to ask to be paid in regular installments, so that they continue to receive paychecks. You need to concentrate on the job of finding a job. That is where you should invest your time and energy. The best way to do this is to keep the rest of your life as normal and stress-free as possible. By receiving regular paychecks for the duration of your severance period—or until you begin a new job—you have one less new thing to wonder or worry about.

If you receive a single, lump-sum payment, by contrast, you have to decide what to do with it. You may have to worry about your tax situation. You may begin to focus on the money and not on your primary target, getting a good new job. You may even move too quickly, taking the wrong job because you want to hang on to as much of the lump sum as you can.

In addition, if you receive a single payment, you are likely to be removed from the company's books immediately. That action normally removes you from health and insurance plans as well. Instead of putting together a solid job campaign, you find yourself shopping for medical coverage. You have more important things to do.

Given the stress associated with losing a job, the chances are better than normal that you might invest your money poorly. One man took his lump-sum severance payment and rushed out to buy a business of his own. He had no experience working on his own, however, and he wasn't equipped to run the business. He stampeded himself into the situation because he was terrified of being without a job. He lost the business, he still needed a job, and he had no money to tide him over during the search.

Somewhat paradoxically, making the decision to go into business for yourself is one of the few instances in which accepting a lump sum can make sense. But be very careful here. If, in the past, you have given considerable thought to the idea of working for yourself and have investigated possibilities and alternatives, or if you have been waiting for an opportunity to head off on your own, now may be the time to act. But be skeptical of your motives if the idea of starting your own business first came to mind after you lost your job. It could be a panic reaction. Reject the possibility outright if you entertain it because you think it may be easier to buy a job than to find one.

The other situation in which a lump-sum payment makes sense occurs when you consider retirement after you have lost a job. If you are nearing retirement age and really *want* to retire, then you will probably wish to invest your severance to supplement the financial arrangements that you've already made for the future. But don't steamroll yourself. A 64-year-old who wants to keep working should go out and find work. A 55-year-old who has wanted to retire for the past ten years should investigate his or her chances of turning that dream into a reality. Control the situation. Don't let it control you.

If you must take your severance in a single payment, see your banker, or broker, or accountant, or tax lawyer, or all four. Get sound advice. You can't be certain how long it will take to find a new job, so now is not the time to invest in cocoa futures. Don't take chances.

And don't expect your former employer to make suggestions about how to handle your money. Companies have landed in court by giving advice that turned out poorly for individuals, who subsequently turned around and sued their former employers.

Remember that, since finding the right job should be the focus of *all* your activity, arranging your financial matters so that they don't intrude on the time you devote to your job search should be an immediate priority. If you are offered a lump sum, for example, you might be able to trade it for the kind of open-ended severance agreement described above. Suggest to your former employer that you be kept on the payroll for as many pay periods as the lump sum would cover. Then, in exchange for the company's agreement to extend the severance period should the need arise, agree to stop receiving payments once you start a new job, even if you are still owed additional severance. You may convince your former employer that you aren't trying to make money at the company's expense, but that you want and deserve a tool to help take you to your next job.*

---

* This tactic may work in another situation, too. Among firms which pay severance in regular installments, some companies stop these payments when an individual takes a new job, but others continue payments for the full severance period, even though a former employee finds a new job sooner. If you find yourself in this latter category, consider negotiating the kind of swap described above.

Other Practical Concerns

You may find that you have to resolve practical matters in addition to the severance agreement. If you had a company car, can you keep it for a while? If you were given a club membership as part of your employment package, how long can you continue to use it? These questions are not as frivolous as they sound. Just as you don't want to spend your time worrying about money, you don't want to divert yourself by searching for a new car. If a club membership was valuable to you in your last job, it will continue to be valuable to you—and to your family—in your present situation.

There may be additional financial topics to consider. If you were covered by a pension fund or profit-sharing plan at your last job, you will need to discover whether you are owed any benefits, and then you will have to decide what to do with them. Once again, professional guidance and a conservative investment approach are probably good ideas at this time.

You should also determine whether your severance package contains any additional benefits that will help you proceed with your job search. Will the company give you outplacement counseling? The process will certainly help as you conduct your campaign. Will office space or secretarial help be provided by your former employer?

Consider your family's needs as you sort through these practical and financial questions. Suppose you and your family have spent the past six months planning and anticipating a vacation that is scheduled to start next Saturday. Consider how canceling it might affect them and, as a result, yourself. Unless your financial investigation has indicated that you are in dire straits, go ahead and take the vacation. It will reduce stress all around. (But if you haven't scheduled a vacation, don't plan one now. You may be trying to evade your current situation.)

Meeting Your Former Employer

After you have considered these topics, you should determine whether you need to arrange another meeting with your former employer. If you didn't discuss your severance package on the day that you were terminated, if you don't understand all its details, or if you think that you should try to negotiate a settlement different from that which was offered to you, go ahead and set up the appointment.

You may also find it important psychologically to face the person who fired you and find out why it happened. If your former boss is willing to see you (some companies discourage second meetings), that's a good sign. He or she will probably be supportive concerning your future needs.

On the other hand, if you *do* understand your termination package, and if you feel that you can live with it, then you may not want a second meeting. It could be explosive, and you don't need any more fireworks.

Moving Ahead

Finally, to discover whether you are ready to move to the next stage of the job search process, ask yourself this question: "What's my problem?"

If you answer, "I just lost my job," you haven't finished dealing with the past. If you say, "I need a new job," you're ready to get organized and set a target for your next job.

4 * Organizing and Targeting

W<small>HEN</small> you shift your attention from the loss of one job to the search for another, you will sooner or later wonder, "Will I *ever* find another job?"

Your concern is natural, but you've asked the wrong question. You will get a new job. The challenge is to find the right job. To succeed at that process, you must catalog and organize your resources, target your search, and plan your campaign.

Many people do not. In the rush to "hit the ground running," they neglect to choose a destination—or even a direction—before they begin their travels. Getting any job, as quickly as possible, becomes the single goal of the job search. Planning doesn't earn a role in the employment campaign.

Planning, in fact, is the weakest part of most careers, as people slip and slide from one job to the next. Have you, for instance, ever taken a full, eight-hour day to think about your career? Or, like most of us, have you spent your working life agreeing to, rather than selecting, the direction your career will take?

It doesn't have to be that way. Now—perhaps for the first time in your career—you have an opportunity to sit back and reflect on who you are and what you want from a job. By matching your personal interests with your professional skills, you can target a job search that considers both.

You might end up with a new career. We worked with one man who lost a job directing the sales force of a huge company. When he probed his interests, he realized that he had always wanted to be a professional athlete. Even without considering his athletic skills, however, there was not much chance that he would get that wish: The man was 40 years old, an unlikely age for rookies in most paying sports.

But 40 is not an unlikely age for rookies in the *business* of sports. Our client discovered that the owners of many professional teams do not run their clubs. They need professional managers to look after their interests. Figuring out that he could apply his business experience to his interest in athletics, our client ultimately took a management position with a pro hockey team, and his avocation became his vocation.

Another client, a 60-year-old man who had been the general manager of a technical firm, was a brilliant scientist but a poor manager. Nevertheless, when he started the outplacement counseling process, he was determined to rush out and land another general manager's post.

We asked whether that was what he really wanted to do with his life. "No," he said, "I'd really like to teach, but it doesn't pay enough."

We had the man figure out how much income his early retirement package would deliver. Then we got him to add in a standard teacher's salary. Finally we suggested that he tack on a figure reflecting the amount he might realistically receive from writing and consulting when he wasn't actually teaching. He learned that he most certainly could afford to do what he had always wanted, and he did. But this highly educated man would never have worked out that simple equation on his own. He had simply assumed that no options existed.

We counseled a woman who lost a job working high above Park Avenue in the market research department of a major consumer corporation. She found out that she really wanted to be in a garage. Her father had been an automobile mechanic, and when she let herself admit the fact, she realized that she had been most satisfied when she had worked alongside him. She is now one of the happiest mechanics in New Jersey, where she runs her own automotive repair shop.

You might learn what *not* to do with your life. One of our clients came out of the food industry and was intrigued by the record business. He investigated the field and discovered that it was characterized by ups, downs, and a general lack of employment security. He also investigated his own needs, learning that he would be happiest in a steadier work environment. He eventually returned to the food business.

You might decide to stick with your present career. Most of our clients do end up taking jobs that are similar to their previous positions. Since so many terminations are caused by reasons that are not connected to performance problems—cutbacks and chemistry issues, for example—that makes sense. If you possess and enjoy using the skills that your last job demanded, performing the same work in a new environment may solve your career dilemma.

But planning is still important, both to identify the proper work environment and to make certain that a more substantial change wouldn't be in your best interests. Finally, if you decide to remain in your present field, you still deserve to plan your future.

We spend a good deal of our time telling people that they deserve to work at things they enjoy. Everyone agrees, and we suspect that no one really believes us. One problem is that so many people continue to insist that you can't call something work unless it hurts.

But many people fear the process of self-investigation that lets them discover what to do with their lives. They're not sure that poking around among skills and needs is such a good idea. What if they find that they don't have any? What if they discover that the situation is worse than even *they* imagined? Both are unlikely, of course, but an individual who has just lost a job often thinks that he's been told, "You're not much good." Real or imagined, the message can lend a terrible logic to either question.

Even people who are willing to consider their own needs often short-circuit the process by getting tangled in the "but" game:

- I always thought of doing that, but I'm not getting any younger.

- Sales management might be perfect for me, but I've invested 12 years in this field.

- Sure I'd love to be a teacher, but I really can't afford it.

The way out of the "but" game is to turn it around on itself. Reverse the clauses: "I've invested 12 years in this field, but sales management might be perfect for me."

To start the planning process, take the energy that tells you that it won't help or that you don't need it, and turn that around on itself, too.

Practical Plans

Start small, if that makes things easier. Plan the nuts-and-bolts aspect of your job search. If your former employer hasn't provided office space and secretarial support for you, or if you won't be using the facilities of an OPC (outplacement counseling) firm during your search, set up your own office. Find a place where you can concentrate and work, without interruption, day after day. If you have an office in your home, so much the better. But a corner of your bedroom will serve your purposes, and headquarters for many a successful job search has been a dining room table.

You'll need a telephone, of course, and you'll have to arrange to have it answered when you're not available. You might consider buying an answering machine or subscribing to an answering service for a few months. If you can't type, find a person or agency to help with letters and other documents.

Once you've put your office together, set a daily schedule for using it. Plan to start work at the same time each morning, just as you would at any other job. Plan your days like regular business days. That's what they are, after all.

If you can't think of immediate projects to tackle, visit your local library to familiarize yourself with business directories and other tools and resources. (Lists are provided in Appendix.) Or go to a stockbroker's office to read annual reports and 10-K statements of companies that interest you. Begin to be active.

References and the Reference Statement

Securing references is an important aspect of the planning and organizing process that you should deal with immediately. The key to making references work for you is to control the story right from the start, even if you think that weeks may pass before your former employer will begin to receive inquiries about you. If you wait to settle the reference question, some other person—or persons—will create a story for you, and it may not be a good one. People abhor vacuums and often fill them with rumors.

We find that references are checked about 70% of the time. And when companies try to fill positions above the $50,000 salary level, our experience shows that the references of leading candidates are contacted about 95% of the time. When they check references, potential employers look for confirmation: They want to find out whether your story—as you've presented it through your résumé or in an interview—is consistent with what your references say about you. You need to make certain that what others say about you doesn't conflict with what you say about yourself.

Identify Candidates. To do this, we suggest that you draft your own reference statement, bearing in mind that you may have to alter it or create separate versions that will be acceptable to a few key people. You will be amazed to discover that the things you've written turn out to be the things that are said about you. Your story becomes the official story, even within your former company.

The first rule is to limit your references to three or four carefully chosen individuals. By controlling the number of people who discuss you with potential employers, you limit the chances that misstatements or damaging remarks will be made. And since you obviously don't want someone who bears you a grudge to be involved in your job search, you choose these people carefully.*

The first exception to the first rule is that, even if you and your ex-boss parted company on miserable terms, you have to include him as a reference. If a potential employer checks references, he'll want to talk with your former boss whether or not you've listed him. If a would-be employer does not plan to contact your references, omitting your last boss from the list might prompt a call to him anyway, as your potential future boss tries to find out why your previous boss *wasn't* listed. In either case, all you've done is raise a bright red flag.

So you'll have to try to reach an agreement on your reference statement with your former boss, whether or not you particularly want to. If you aren't successful you will at least know what to expect from him in the future. Remember that people who check references are seeking confirmation. If you believe that they will hear something bad about you, warn them first. You might say, "I should tell you that my former boss and I had a number of disagreements. She

---

* You should be warned that people who play heavy roles in terminations occasionally feel determined to justify the decision. They may work subtly and even unconsciously to keep the person who lost the job from replacing it with a better position. If you suspect this kind of behavior, avoid the individual as a reference.

stuck to her guns, I stuck to mine, and neither of us kept our thoughts a secret from the other." If your former boss then says, "We fought tooth and nail," all she has done is confirm your story. A potential employer who is sufficiently impressed with your qualifications to check your references is likely to go elsewhere for a third opinion. On the other hand, if you say, "We got along just fine," and your ex-boss says, "We fought tooth and nail," then you're in trouble.

Since you have more latitude in the choice of your other references, you should not have this problem with them. But before you select anyone as a reference, try to determine what he or she is likely to say about you. The immediate superior of your former boss might be a good reference, for example, but only if he knows you and your work well enough to discuss you intelligently. You've only flown another scarlet flag if a reference you've named tells an inquiring employer, "Gee, I don't know what to tell you. I really don't know the guy too well."

On the other hand, if you suspect that your previous boss will give you a bad report, his boss might act as an arbiter or referee and bring a sense of perspective to the situation. That could make him a valuable reference.

You might choose someone from an earlier point in your career. Once again, though, don't pretend that your favorite boss can take the place of your most recent boss, unless they are the same person. Most of your references should come from your most recent company.

Other possibilities include a peer or even a former subordinate. Here as well, give some thought to what you think either might say about you. We counseled one man, a top executive, and watched as he almost landed, but narrowly missed out on, offers for three excellent jobs. Contacts at the companies finally told us that, in each case, he had been done in by a former coworker who said, "He's a great guy, but don't let him near your company." That "friend" cost our client three job offers. Our client hadn't thought it necessary to nail down an agreement on his story.

How to Draft the Statement. When you have identified your candidates for references, draft the reference statement itself. Be credible, positive, clear, and concise. Make the statement no longer than a page. If you can compress the story to a single paragraph while covering the following points, do so.

First, tell how this reference knows you. What was your reporting relationship? Are you personal friends as well as business acquaintances?

Next, discuss your skills and accomplishments. What things did you do especially well at your previous job? What contributions did you make to the company? (For guidance, see the section "The Personal Assessment.")

Mention personal traits next. What kind of a manager are you? Participative? Autocratic? Refer to a management style. Describe your rapport with other employees at the firm. Represent yourself as a stable manager. Don't discuss personality conflicts, even if they were a problem at your last job. A good interviewer will jump all over a statement like, "He had trouble with some members of his department." Your reference will be asked, "Was he a hard person to manage?" or, "Did he go off half-cocked?" Don't help create a questionable environment.

You may decide to include a carefully thought-out negative about yourself, however. Choose a minor weakness that could be considered a strength carried a bit too far: "He goes at his work so hard that he sometimes steps on toes." But show that you are working to improve the trait: "He recognizes and is working to correct the situation."

Finally, tell why you left the job.* Think this through, because you will have to live with it in the future. And keep it brief: You, not one of your references, should be the only

---

* If you haven't made your termination public, tell why you're *leaving* your job. But be careful here. Make sure your reference will agree with you. Say something like, "He is still on the payroll [you are if you receive regular severance payments], but he has decided, and the company has agreed, that he should spend the majority of his time on his job search."

person to get involved in a detailed discussion of the subject.

If your termination was caused by a reorganization or staff reduction, you might give either as the reason for leaving your job, but you could also turn the situation to your advantage: "When he finished the assignment, he looked for other opportunities within the company, found none that matched his needs and fit his plans, and decided to look outside the firm." Position yourself as having taken the initiative to further your own career. Advertise yourself as the director of this production, not the audience.

In many situations, the best explanation is a variation on the "We agreed to disagree" theme: "He didn't feel that the company's plans matched his own, and we agreed that his best option would be to search out an opportunity closer to his own needs." Make the statement sound like an honest and understandable difference of opinion. Don't try to prove that you were right and they were wrong. Suggest that you decided, through a rational thought process, to find another position better suited to your interests and abilities.

Review the Statement with Your Key References.   When you complete the reference statement, you need to review it with the people you've identified as references so that they will agree to stick with your story. At the outset, you may doubt your ability to reach such an agreement, but unless you have pillaged or plundered at your last job, you'll probably find that people at the company are willing and even anxious to work something out. Remember that companies, or more accurately the people who run them, are growing more and more likely to accept some blame when terminations occur. If you weren't successful at your job, they weren't successful at their jobs. Even if your former boss feels that the decision to terminate you was entirely justified, he probably feels some guilt about the situation. He fired you, but it is unlikely that he wants you to hate him. It is equally unlikely that he wants to ruin your life; he may even want to help. Try to seek an agreement in a friendly manner.

But no matter what happens, don't get lured into an

argument. Remember to do what's best for you. If someone reads your reference statement and says, "That's not at all the way it happened," be prepared with a response like, "There are probably as many opinions of what happened here as there are people who were involved in the decision. But what I need to do is to settle on some simple statement that we can all live with." Talk like that, and they'll wonder why they fired you.

Be willing to compromise. Start with as positive a statement as you can reasonably create, but be prepared to discuss alternatives if one of your references says, "I just can't go along with that." It's ideal to unite your references in a chorus of praise, but it's more important that not one of them says, "He messed up left and right."

Suppose that you can reach agreement on this statement:

He was an effective manager in the field of communications, he managed a staff of forty people, and he reported directly to me. He did this job with us for six years. He left the company because he saw the business heading in one direction, we saw it moving in another, and he thought that his career should take him along different paths than ours.

That isn't the most inspiring reference statement of all time, but you should be able to live with it. It describes someone who did a job effectively and stood up for his own needs and ideas. Compare it with another possibility: "He wasn't on the team, and we just couldn't use him anymore." That kind of statement surfaces when you don't plan and control your references.

You should also realize that companies are much more reluctant today about giving out personal information than they were in the past. Managers worry about legal repercussions should something be said that cannot be proved. If a company spokesman tells a potential employer that you were "fired," for instance, when technically you were asked to resign and did so, the company may find itself on shaky legal footing. As "freedom of information" legislation allows individuals access to things that are said about them, institutions limit their comments. As one observer has noted, "If your termination policies won't stand up in court, you will."

Some companies give out very little information about former employees: the fact that they did work for the firm, the dates they were employed, the title of the job or jobs they held, and perhaps their salaries. This corporate tendency to limit the flow of information may help you reach agreement on another matter. When you discuss your reference statement with individuals at your former company, ask that only the people you've identified as references be allowed to discuss your record and qualifications when would-be employers contact the firm. Management won't have to worry that someone might make an ill-advised remark which lands the firm in court, and you will have limited the number of commentators to the individuals with whom you've reached an agreement.

If you need a final reassuring thought about references and reference checking, consider this: Search firms, which often handle the reference checking process, earn their substantial fees by filling jobs. If they think that you are a good candidate for a position, they want to market you. That desire can affect the vigor with which they investigate your references. This fact of business life led to an interesting situation not long ago. A television network retained two search firms to fill one top-level job. Part of the arrangement was that each firm was responsible for checking the references of candidates raised by the other.

Vocational Testing

After you deal with the question of references (or, even better, while you're handling references), you should also think about vocational and aptitude testing, another useful part of the planning and organizing phase of your job search. Taking a battery of tests and discussing the results with a competent counselor supplies valuable objective data about job-related strengths and weaknesses, defines areas in which you might profit from further development, and gives clues about career directions that are likely to mesh with your skills and interests.

We urge all our clients to take advantage of the vocational review process. Soon after they begin outplacement counseling, in fact, most spend four to six hours taking a series of tests and discussing the results with one of our staff psychologists. Almost all the participants discover that the process helps them define new career opportunities. Most refer back to their test results throughout their employment campaigns.

Yet even intelligent people sometimes balk at the idea of testing. Businessmen who wouldn't dream of signing a contract without calling in their lawyers; investors who wouldn't invest in a haircut without consulting their tax accountants; and public figures who won't repeat their own names without talking to public relations advisers are occasionally unwilling to accept expert help when the subject turns to a much more important topic—their own futures.

If you feel the same way, here are answers to some considerations that may trouble you: No one will tell you what to do with your life. You won't be brainwashed. You won't need a new, and smaller, hat after the testing session. You won't learn that you should have been a longshoreman or a stock clerk all along (unless those are jobs that you've wanted all along).

What you are likely to be is reassured. The tests usually confirm feelings that you have had about your interests. They may help you avoid repeating past mistakes and point you toward a better work climate in the future. They often crystallize hazy thoughts and ideas about your future. And, particularly if you are running your job search without the help of professional outplacement counselors, the test results act as a yardstick or sounding board against which you can measure hypotheses and consider options.

Before you begin the testing process, you need to answer one important question: How do you make certain that the counselor who administers and interprets the tests is competent and trustworthy? Anyone, unfortunately, can award himself the title, "Career Guidance Counselor." The only necessary qualification is the ability to write an ad or hang out a shingle.

Personal referrals are probably the best way to locate a good counselor. Business schools or graduate schools of psychology may have referral services. Your family doctor may know a good vocational counselor. The director of personnel or human resources management at your former company might be able to direct you to a proven counselor. An acquaintance who has gone through the job search process may be able to help. If you know a psychologist or psychiatrist, ask for advice.

It may help to look for professional credentials and seek a board-certified, Ph.D. psychologist. But make sure that the individual's degree is in counseling or industrial psychology, not in linguistics, child psychology, or any other specialty not directly related to your needs. And remember that degrees don't make people competent; ability and experience do.

At any rate, don't spend too much time agonizing over the selection. You deserve to find a competent, trustworthy counselor since you are dealing with important personal information. But the tests are relatively straightforward, and your counselor doesn't have to be a genius to interpret the results.

The Personal Assessment

Testing is an extremely useful organizing tool, but the real key to the planning process is the personal assessment: an inventory of what you've done (your accomplishments); what you can do (your skills); and what you'd like to do (your interests). Listing your career accomplishments allows you to identify your skills. Examining your skills and interests lets you determine what you would like to do, as well as where and with whom you would like to do it. By combining all this information, you can target your job search, narrowing your campaign to a particular industry, a part of an industry, or, ideally, a specific group of companies or institutions that particularly appeal to you.

What You've Done

Organizations hire people they think will make contributions to the company by accomplishing tasks and solving problems. You must be able to convince potential employers that you possess the skills and the experience to do both. To achieve that, you need to be aware of your own accomplishments.

Throughout your career, you have undoubtedly done many things that have been important to the organizations you've worked for. But some of these successes may only have been noted briefly, as you hurried on to your next task. Others may not have been identified at all. Even *you* may have failed to recognize the things that you've done and neglected to understand how well they illustrate your skills and abilities. Since these accomplishments are the best possible evidence of your skill at working effectively, you should pinpoint them now, so that you can advertise them throughout your job search.

Make a list of personal accomplishments that go back to the beginning of your career. Don't be too discriminating at first; list everything that comes up. Toot your own horn. Don't limit yourself by thinking, "Well, I really didn't do it all by myself." Very few people ever did. Come up with at least twenty-five examples, and try to list forty or fifty. Include accomplishments from all the positions you've held, but concentrate on your most recent jobs. Include accomplishments from your personal life if you feel that they help define who you are, such as your work in a volunteer organization. (If you have not been working long enough to have accumulated many accomplishments, examples from your personal life are particularly important.)

As you build your list, keep a couple of guidelines in mind. State accomplishments crisply and briefly. Specify the result or impact that each example had on the organization. Don't be too general. Whenever you can, measure results in numerical or percentage terms. If you increased productivity, how great was the increase? If you cut costs, tell by how much. A well-stated accomplishment will describe what you did and give a tangible measurement of its result to the company.

Generally, an activity is an accomplishment if it satisfies one or more of these criteria:

- It achieved more with the same resources.
- It made things simpler or easier.
- It resolved a problem with little or no increase in time, effort, money, or personnel.
- It did something useful for the first time.

In most cases, results generated by accomplishments fit one of the following categories (but keep in mind that these values should be quantified whenever possible):

- Increased profits
- Increased sales
- Reduced costs
- Enlarged market or share
- Improved quality
- Improved employee relations
- Improved productivity and teamwork
- Reduced operations time
- Achieved or established a technological process
- Identified a need or problem before it became obvious

- Planned a program from scratch
- Implemented or controlled an important program or action

As you list accomplishments, don't write phrases like "was responsible for" or "was involved with." Use action verbs like these:

Accomplished	Headed	Redesigned
Achieved	Implemented	Reduced
Approved	Improved	Reorganized
Arbitrated	Improvised	Researched
Built	Increased	Resolved
Completed	Installed	Revised
Conceived	Innovated	Scheduled
Conducted	Instituted	Serviced
Consolidated	Introduced	Setup
Constructed	Invented	Simplified
Controlled	Launched	Sold
Converted	Led	Solved
Created	Maintained	Sparked
Cut	Managed	Staffed
Decreased	Narrowed	Started
Delivered	Negotiated	Streamlined
Demonstrated	Operated	Strengthened
Designed	Organized	Stressed
Developed	Originated	Stretched
Devised	Performed	Structured
Directed	Planned	Succeeded
Doubled	Prevented	Superseded
Earned	Processed	Supervised
Edited	Produced	Terminated
Eliminated	Promoted	Traced
Established	Proposed	Tracked
Expanded	Provided	Traded
Founded	Purchased	Trained
Generated	Recommended	Transferred

Transformed	Unified	Widened
Translated	Unraveled	Won
Trimmed	Utilized	Withdrew
Tripled	Vacated	Worked
Uncovered	Verified	Wrote

You may have to rewrite each statement several times before you are satisfied with it. In the following descriptive list of solid accomplishments, some statements are more specific than others, but all aim for precision and clarity:

- Created a profit and loss statement, by product, which resulted in dropping 20% of product line that was found to be unprofitable.
- Developed premiums and reserves for Accidental Death and Guaranteed Insurability benefits for a new rate manual.
- Conceived a new management information services procedure which made vital operation reports available to management the following day instead of at the end of the week.
- Prepared payroll manually, converted to punch cards, entered on disc, and transmitted to data center.
- Through reorganization and introduction of methods and systems, reduced rework by 3%, eliminated schedule delays, and tripled in-house manufacturing capability.
- Conducted studies and negotiated contracts with outside vendors for office equipment.
- Designed supporting equipment and techniques for a new process that raised product market potential from $50 million to over $200 million per year.
- Saved up to $3 million in possible damages, and prevented embarrassment, by discovering potential bankruptcy for a supplier.
- Found $190,000 overstatement of a division's inventory, enabling corrective action by management.

- Initiated procedures to increase production 100% by reducing turn-around time from 5–6 days to 1–2 days.
- Reduced turnover of personnel from 17% to 9% per year.
- Proved that a $2.2 million inventory shortage predated the acquisition of a division.
- Developed a community acceptance campaign in San Francisco (a hostile market) resulting in a 40% gain in the Bay Area.
- Implemented a work load report by consultant, showing all pertinent client information.
- Instituted a wage and salary program especially tailored to improve morale while eliminating waste, reducing payroll by $1,000,000.
- Analyzed statistical reports to pinpoint errors and develop new procedures to improve system.
- Developed and installed a unique laboratory organization that eliminated duplication, encouraged cooperation, and reduced costs by $100,000.
- Developed responses to press inquiries and prepared position statements for the company's top executives.
- As corporate officer of a multi-million dollar non-profit tax-exempt corporation, cut operation expenses by 12% and increased efficiency.
- Conducted studies on duplicating equipment, time-sharing terminals and telephones, saving $45,000/yr. through a reduction in manpower and equipment.
- Negotiated the acquisition of $1,500,000 worth of valuable patents from a billion dollar company in exchange for an equity position resulting in a gain of $2,000,000.
- Initiated and directed a Community Services Program which processed within twenty-four hours every citizen complaint or request and incorporated a complete training program for future public administrators.

As you create your list of personal accomplishments, you are likely to discover that the process makes you feel good about yourself. It should. You may never have realized just how many useful things you've done in your working career. But because the process does make you feel comfortable, you may find yourself saying, "I think I'll just keep on listing things." During this—or any—mechanical phase of the job search process, think about timing. Don't move forward too quickly, but don't get stuck anywhere along the way. You can always change the personal assessment later in your search, but you should have finished a good working document within a week.

Also, don't sell yourself short, but don't overstate your accomplishments, either. If you left college three years ago, if your most recent job title was "assistant brand manager," and if one of your accomplishments is, "Introduced a new personal care product that captured a 14% market share in its first year," you'd better be able to prove the fact. A statement like, "Scheduled and tested the market introduction of a personal care product that . . ." might serve you better when you write a résumé or discuss accomplishments during a job interview several weeks or months from now. Be accurate.

What You Can Do

When you have completed your list of accomplishments, you will have created an inventory of the things you have done during your career. Next, you need to create a list of the things you *can* do—your skills and abilities. Review your list of accomplishments and identify the dominant skills you used to achieve each of them. These abilities are more general than the accomplishments they produce, but don't let yourself be too vague or hazy as you list them. Avoid ambiguous terms and clichés. Don't write, "I am strong on leadership," or, "I get along well with people," or, "I command loyalty." Don't say what you are; stick to phrases that show what you can do. It isn't a real skill unless it lets you do something actively.

This list of key words and phrases defines a variety of specific skills and abilities:

- Analyzing
- Artistic, Design
- Communicating, Verbal, Persuasive (speeches, presentations, teaching, languages)
- Conceptualizing
- Coordinating, Liaison
- Creating, Organizing (ideas, new approaches)
- Data, Details (figures, records, systems, controls, research)
- Judging, Decision making, Intuition
- Leading, Directing, Motivating, Supervising
- Listening
- Mechanical, Manual
- Memory
- Negotiating
- Observing
- Organizing
- Planning
- Problem solving, identifying
- Synthesizing

What You Would Like To Do

After you have sifted through your list of career accomplishments to identify the skills you have used in the past, you are ready to consider the third side of the personal assessment triangle: what you would like to do in the future.

Some people choose a career at an early age, pursuing it with enthusiasm and satisfaction for a lifetime. Who hasn't heard of the surgeon who realized that he wanted to be a doctor when he was six years old? Who hasn't read about an actress who staged her first basement production at age five and never looked back?

But it is much more common for people to select a general field of education, stumble into a first job without much planning or foresight, and then continue along that track throughout their careers. If they are lucky, the requirements of their jobs coincide with their abilities and desires. But, frequently, their work does not have a great deal to do with their skills and interests. What they do is determined by superiors who have their own sets of priorities to consider.

Even people who plan their careers carefully find that needs and interests can change during the course of a working lifetime. Some people adapt: Dentists—even dentists who chose their careers at age seven—become real estate developers; real estate developers become teachers; teachers become stockbrokers. But many people never choose new career paths to fit their changing personal interests. Then, ten, twenty, or even thirty years into their careers, they discover that they no longer enjoy going to work. Perhaps the job has grown too stressful. Perhaps it has become boring and repetitive. Perhaps a career has taken the person in a direction he or she does not enjoy. Perhaps the field itself is no longer expanding and, as a result, offers limited future opportunity for personal and professional growth.

Targeting

Right now, you can find out whether you are on the career track that suits you best. By looking at work-related elements which bring you real satisfaction, you can determine the kind of challenges and the working environment that are most likely to let you operate happily and successfully.

You've already done most of the homework for this exercise in self-understanding: The items that show up most frequently on your lists of accomplishments and skills are likely to reflect values that are closely related to your perception of enjoyment and satisfaction. People tend to perform best doing the things they like most. You probably like to do things that you do well and do well at things you enjoy.

Choose three or four positions—not necessarily in order of personal preference—that you've held in recent years. For each job, write down as many things as you can that you found attractive or stimulating about the position—things that you enjoyed doing. Then write down the things that you did not enjoy—unpleasant duties, disagreeable relationships, or unacceptable pressures, for example. Looking at all the positives and negatives that you identify, make a personal summary of things that make a job satisfying to you and items that make a position unattractive. Refer to both sets of conclusions as you consider career options.

But don't just look to the past for inspiration about the future. You may possess additional skills and interests that haven't been called upon recently. Your interests may prompt you to learn new skills. You may want to enter an entirely new field. As the case histories mentioned at the beginning of this chapter indicate, many of our clients consider such radical career changes.

If such an idea brings a gleam to your eye, try to describe your "dream" job as fully and as specifically as you can. What pluses and minuses do you think might be associated with it?

Let your imagination roam as you consider these possibilities. Be a little outlandish. Don't put a damper on your thoughts just yet. If you have a favorite pastime, for instance, consider whether you might enjoy working at it full time.

Once you've fantasized about possibilities, examine their practicality. Could you establish credibility for yourself in an entirely new field? Perhaps some of your skills are transferable. Maybe you have a friend in the field who believes in your ability.

If compensation in a new career would be substantially below what you are currently used to, could you adapt, or would you and your family's lifestyle suffer too greatly? Think back to the manager who "couldn't afford" to be a teacher before you answer that question.

Your daydreams may involve starting your own business. Will you be able to finance it? Do you know enough about the new business to compete successfully?

Is there a logical connection between your interests and a new career? The fact that you enjoy eating in restaurants, for example, doesn't mean that you should open one. (Do you really want to spend Sunday mornings making zucchini quiche?) The fact that you love weekend golf may be caused by the fact that you only have to play it on weekends. Turning a hobby into a job can take away most of the fun.

If these kinds of practical questions don't shake your faith in the idea of a radical career change, investigate the new field closely. Put together all the information you can assemble. Check brokerage houses for research reports on industries or companies that operate in the new field. Talk to people who work in the business. Locate recent articles on the field in business magazines and journals. Attend conferences or conventions related to the new area that interests you. As you learn more about the field, you will get closer to an educated decision about whether you should become involved in it. If you decide to make a radical career shift, the information that you've dug up through research will let you speak intelligently with potential employers in the new field and may convince them that you are both serious about making the change and sufficiently skilled to do so.

We worked with one man who lost an important job in consumer marketing. He looked around and decided that cable television would be just the place for him. At first, we weren't convinced. Too many people, it seemed, imagine that salvation lurked somewhere in the cable TV business. We wondered whether our client, with his background, should seriously contemplate such a move.

But he was persistent, studying the cable industry in remarkable detail. He read everything he could find, talked to everyone he could locate, and gave a great deal of careful thought to the industry. He became mesmerized by the opportunities and possibilities he discovered. He ended up with an exceptionally thorough market study of the cable business. It convinced him (and us, finally) that he should adopt it for himself. He now occupies a senior position in the cable TV industry.

When he finished his job search, he told us that this planning and targeting phase of the OPC process had clearly been the most important ingredient of his employment campaign. Without it, he said, he doubted whether he would have made the decision to head in the direction he took and whether he would have been taken seriously when he searched for a job in the field.

Your investigation of a new career may bring different results, however. You may conclude that you shouldn't make a radical change—at least not just yet. You might convince yourself to start planning, training, and saving to switch at a later date. Perhaps you are one job away from your dream job.

Or you may discover that you really don't want to change careers, even if you didn't enjoy your most recent job. You may discover that something in your personal life makes it difficult for you to enjoy your work. The industry you've worked in—not the duties you performed—may disagree with you. The work environment at a particular company may have been the problem. Any of these is an important discovery. If something tripped you up in the past, it's likely to snare you again in the future, unless you change either your own habits or the environment in which you work.

Most of our clients reestablish themselves in positions similar to their previous jobs with organizations similar to their previous companies. They find that it is easier to find a job in a field in which they have a track record and that it is also easier to maintain or improve their income in fields where they have established themselves. By taking part in the planning process, however, they get the satisfaction of having considered alternatives and found them less intriguing than their own professions. They also learn what makes a job satisfying for them.

So the important thing to do is to create a target. If,

when you are finished, you find your present occupation is in the bull's-eye, then you're in fine shape. But what if no well-defined areas or industries come to mind? What can you do?

Try to narrow the field by asking yourself a series of questions that will help you limit your search.

First, what kind of organization do you think you would like to work for? Consider these variables:

- Profit or nonprofit?
- Retail or wholesale?
- Industrial or consumer?
- Manufacturing, processing, distributing, or service?
- Domestic or international?
- Federal, state, or local government?
- Church?
- Public, private, or your own company?
- Centralized or decentralized?
- Large, medium, or small organization?

Second, do you have any geographical preferences? Are any locations totally unacceptable to you?

Third, what sort of working climate appeals to you? Do you prefer a relaxed environment, or do you need constant activity or a crisis atmosphere to keep you interested?

Include your family in this question-and-answer exercise. Get agreement on such matters as geographical location, work patterns, or travel requirements. Don't assume that your spouse will follow you blindly. What are your children's needs? Does your spouse have a job which he or she may be willing to leave? Don't imagine that you are the center of the universe. People pay heavily for those assumptions.

Be honest with yourself as you answer these questions. Many of our clients lose jobs because they think they should be in an aggressive environment but cannot really handle the stress and, worst of all, don't really enjoy the pressure.

They've read too many business magazine articles about superaggressive managers. On the other hand, if you really *are* an aggressive person, admit it and find a job where the trait will be welcome. Or, if you care about family life, realize that the need must enter your planning process. A twenty-four-hour-a-day job simply won't work for you.

A Weighted Approach to Targeting

The chart on the opposite page represents a systematic, numerically weighted grid approach to targeting. Using it, you can identify what is important to you in a job and, later in your job search, when you consider particular fields or companies, you can determine how well they match your plans. For now, however, think about your needs (column 1).

Consider the criteria on the chart. Rank each item using a scale of 1 (least important to you) to 10 (most important to you). Take the criteria "Promotion/Personal Growth Potential" as an example. Suppose that the ability to move up in a company is extremely important to you. You might put a 10 in column 1. As you investigate career options, this will remind you to be especially observant of the chances, or lack of chances, various companies or organizations provide for advancement.

Suppose you put a 2 in the "My Needs" column opposite the "Size of Company" criterion. That indicates that the size of the company you work for is not important to you. You can, as a result, virtually disregard this factor as you plan your search.

When you have finished filling in the boxes for all sixteen criteria, you will have a handy set of guidelines that will help you plan your search. If you awarded "Geographic Location" a ten, for instance, indicating that where you work is particularly important to you, you'll have focused your search dramatically. Perhaps you won't even consider jobs located outside your preferred geographical area. That will simplify your planning considerably; on the other hand, of course, it

CAREER TARGETING GRID

CRITERIA	My Needs	Company A		Company B		Company C	
	(1)	(2)	(1)x(2)	(3)	(1)x(3)	(4)	(1)x(4)
CAREER/PROFESSIONAL FACTORS							
Accountability							
Adequacy of Staff							
Title							
Promotion/Personal Growth Potential							
Decision-making Authority							
COMPANY FACTORS							
Size of Company							
Company/Industry History Characteristics							
Management Style (Participative, Autocratic, etc.)							
PERSONAL FACTORS							
Compensation Base							
Bonus/Profit-sharing/ Stock Options							
Benefits (Pension, Disability, Life Insurance, Vacation)							
Perks (Car, Country Club, etc.)							
Geographic Location							
Travel Requirements							
Commuting Requirements							
Special Expenses (Commuting Fares, Taxes, Relocation, etc.)							
TOTAL SCORES							

may complicate your job search by limiting your opportunities. But if location is extremely important to you, you
should recognize and respond to that fact.

If, as you move through the job search process, you discover that your needs are changing—so that what originally
seemed important no longer appears to be quite so critical—
you can refer back to this chart and change your rankings
accordingly. But be as honest as you can with yourself, now
and in the future. If decision-making authority is very important to you now (you gave it a 9 perhaps), don't convince
yourself in two months that it is not so very important simply
because you haven't found a job offering much authority in
the interim. Be sensitive to your needs and trust them.

Targeting is invaluable to the job search process, but
only if you approach it properly. Some people think that
hitting the bull's eye involves grabbing a gun, facing a wall,
closing the eyes, pulling the trigger, and then painting con-
centric circles around the hole that results.

That's not the kind of targeting we've described. Don't
be picked by a job. Don't automatically assume that because
you've done something in the past, or because it's what fast-
track people are doing these days, or because everyone says
there's a future in it, you must convince yourself that a certain job is what you really want to do with your life. Approach the question from the other direction. Discover
what's important to you and then find a job that fills those
needs.

5 ✳ Résumés

MORE talk—and less sense—is devoted to résumés than to any other topic in most job searches. There is no shortage of experts on the subject and no lack of conflicting opinions about the proper form and actual usefulness of these documents. Some people insist that the résumé is the key to finding a job. Others argue that writing a résumé is unnecessary and perhaps counterproductive.*

Those who discount the importance of résumés say that they are commonplace and ordinary, that they make one résumé-toter indistinguishable from the next, and that, if someone is *really* unique, he or she won't need one to get a job. This line of thought could, we suppose, persuade people to demonstrate their uniqueness by wearing lime green shorts to interviews. It has no doubt prompted a few misguided souls to send out lime green résumés.

People who argue that résumés are the most important piece in the job-hunting puzzle are also likely to feel that job

---

* A few people even find time to worry about the number of acute accents that should be hoisted over the word. "Resume," "resumé" and "résumé" are all acceptable, we feel, so pick a favorite, and, for the sake of consistency, stick with it.

searches begin and end with the distribution of hundreds of résumés to hundreds of companies. At our firm, about one of every ten jobs our clients find does, in fact, result from this sort of mass mailing, but, even then, the résumé doesn't *get* the job, it helps get an interview that leads to an offer for a job.

The trouble with both arguments is that neither addresses the real purpose of the résumé. It is a supplementary tool—and an important one—a personal advertising brochure that lets you communicate with a number of audiences. It doesn't take the place of a marketing strategy, it supports one.

If, for instance, your search plan includes working through executive search firms or placement agencies, they will want to see your résumé. If you answer newspaper and trade journal advertisements, you will normally be asked to send along a résumé. When you start to build a network of personal contacts, you will need to distribute résumés to most of the people you meet along the way. If you send out a mailing to companies, you will usually include a copy of your résumé. In the next chapter, we will discuss each of these marketing strategies and urge that you include all four in your job search. We think that you'll need a good résumé to pursue them effectively.

Résumés serve other purposes, too. They let you organize your career by selecting and presenting events clearly and concisely. This pays dividends later. Without having gone through the process of creating a résumé, many of us would sit in interviews and say, "Let's see, in '65 I was with Monsanto. No, that was in '69. I joined Allied in '62, and in '64 they moved me to San Jose, so by '65 I was probably . . ."

A résumé also lets you emphasize the things that you think are important about you. You create a format of your own choosing and, at many interviews—particularly when you are speaking to an inexperienced interviewer—this format becomes the agenda for the discussion. That's a clear advantage for you, since you have designed the structure of the interview.

You need a résumé at any career level. Whenever one person represents you to someone else, the first question that is likely to be raised is, "Can I see some paper on that person?"

The farther you move up the job pyramid, the more important your résumé becomes. This surprises some people, who think that at the highest levels, the search process is a person-to-person verbal event. On the contrary, even if a board chairman interviews you for a job as president of one of his company's subsidiaries, he'll have to share you throughout his organization: up the line (with his board of directors), across the line (with other senior executives, who may be scattered across the country or around the world) and perhaps even down the line (with some of the people you would manage if you took the job). He'll probably use a memo attached to your résumé to communicate with these people. That should please you, because you will be represented by statements that you've made about yourself. But you'll obviously need a résumé that you feel comfortable with.

The only real problem with résumés is that too many people spend too much time working on them. The process simply isn't complex enough to warrant the obsessive attention it sometimes receives. You should march through the preparation of your résumé, since you've already done most of the work by cataloguing your skills and accomplishments during the targeting phase of your search. Now you need to organize and distill this information, choosing your most important career achievements and listing them clearly and concisely. Your goal is to create an action-oriented digest of your abilities, responsibilities, and accomplishments.

Don't turn résumé-writing into a delaying tactic. Don't spend weeks revising and rewriting as you stalk that mythical beast, the "perfect" résumé. Don't decide that you need to create a separate résumé for each employment opportunity you investigate. Cover letters, which we'll discuss later, will tailor your generic résumé to specific situations.

Make sure that you write your own résumé. You'll have to live with it. If someone else does the job for you, the résumé won't be a part of you; you'll have to sound like it. In an interview, you could find yourself justifying points or explaining matters that never would have surfaced if you had done the job yourself. For the same reason, avoid résumé-writing services, which normally end up as expensive printers anyway, even if they do claim to design layouts (which you can do) and write copy (which you should do).

If you don't think that you write well enough to prepare a good résumé, get a friend with better writing skills to review what you've done. But remember that *everyone* is an expert on résumés. Close friends and casual acquaintances alike will suggest that you move this, rearrange that, or delete both. When people don't know what to tell you about your job search, but think that they ought to say something, they tend to offer advice about résumés. Don't take the bait. Once you are satisfied with it, don't be too quick to reinvent the document unless you discover a major omission or a glaring error.

Résumé Formats

Most résumés follow either a chronological or a functional format. The chronological variety describes your career in reverse chronological order, starting with your most recent job and working back through earlier positions. It discusses your employment history concisely and straightforwardly (or, perhaps, straightbackwardly), tying your skills and accomplishments to the companies you've worked for and the positions you've held.

We recommend that most people write chronological résumés. The individuals who read résumés normally have a number of résumés to consider at one time and appreciate compositions that show them, quickly and clearly, what the individual has done and where he or she has done it. They may not be patient: Rather than search for information, they may discard one résumé and pick up another. For this reason, you need to get your message across quickly and forcefully. A chronological résumé is usually the simplest, most direct means to that end.

But there are situations in which a chronological résumé won't deliver the message that you want sent. Here, a functional résumé may work best. It plays down your actual employment record and stresses a summary of the functions you have performed during your career. If you have an erratic work history, for instance—several jobs in a relatively short time span, perhaps, or a considerable gap between positions—you probably won't want to draw attention to the situation. Or suppose you intend to make a radical career change, and, as a result, the companies you've worked for or the titles you've held don't lend themselves to your new career objective. You'll most likely want to downplay them and emphasize various skills or accomplishments that better support your plans. If your actual work experience is so limited that a chronological résumé might not represent your abilities properly, you won't want to use one. If you intend to return to a previous occupation, you'll want to stress the experience you have in the field rather than raise questions about why you left it and now want to return.

In situations like these, where the accessibility of a chronological résumé—normally its major selling point—hinders rather than helps your cause, think about drafting a functional résumé. But think well, and weigh the fact that some people simply don't like to read functional résumés. If you can, use a chronological format.

Take the time to study the sample résumés that follow. Each is well-planned and well-written. Each speaks in terms of responsibilities and accomplishments. Each strikes a good balance between stressing the needs and goals of the writer and addressing the likely priorities of potential readers.

Consider the style and design of each example. Remember that, once someone picks up a résumé, he may not have—or may not take—much time to pick out its message. These samples show how to use short phrases or sentences to get the message across quickly. They use action verbs and simple language and avoid long, indecipherable paragraphs. Topics and subtopics are carefully arranged in outline form, and bullets or other symbols are used to set one item from another. Enough blank space is left on the pages so that readers aren't overwhelmed with type.

When you write your résumé, remember that simple is usually elegant. Don't get fancy with design elements unless you're looking for work as an art director. You may lack the skills, and your reader may lack the aesthetic sense, that an involved design demands. Don't let anyone think, "If he has to resort to *this*, he must really be in deep trouble."

CHRONOLOGICAL FORMAT

William N. Beetles
89 Rockfile Drive
Frogsneck, MN 15510

Home Phone: (613) 555-0510   Office Phone: (613) 555-6903

OBJECTIVE

To direct the corporate data center of a major enterprise, preferably with significant responsibility in the administrative and corporate planning functions.

BACKGROUND SUMMARY

Over eleven years of results-oriented experience in data center operations. Proven ability to manage and plan a large scale data center operation to support the objectives of a major firm. Hardware experience encompasses AMDAHL V-5, IBM 370/165, 370/158, and 370/145. Software experience includes MVS, VM/CMS, and all versions of O.S., HASP, TSO, and CICS.

BUSINESS EXPERIENCE

UNION LIFE INSURANCE COMPANY   1978 to present

Manager, Computer Operations

Present position includes the administrative and technical responsibility for all computer processing activities of the corporation, as well as responsibility for hardware capacity measurement, change control, problem determination, and site preparation and installation of all hardware. I have the accountability for the preparation and expenditure of an annual operating budget of $3.5 million. Installed hardware consists of a six meg AMDAHL V-5 and a six meg IBM 370/158. Peripheral devices consist of three 3211 printers, eighty (3330/3350) disks, and eighteen tape drives. Software systems utilized are VM, MVS/JES2, CMS, and CICS.

Accomplishments:
- Saved the company $100,000 a year by introducing a competitive terminal to the user community that would provide the same features for less money.
- Introduced an in-house training program to bring staff up to date technically.
- Instituted a management team within the operations area to manage daily activities where none existed before.
- In a year of major changes, was able to stay within my projected budget ($3.5 million) figure and still accomplish objectives.

William N. Beetles   Page 2

PENNSYLVANIA WHITE SHIELD   1974 to 1978

Computer Production Supervisor

Member of the original management team that was recruited to plan, develop, organize, and manage the conversion of health care and financial systems from a facilities management firm to an in-house operation. Directed the scheduling and operation of all production activities through a staff of thirty-three. Accountable for the preparation and expenditure of an annual operating budget of $2 million.

Accomplishments:

- Converted first major application forty-five days ahead of schedule. Resulted in an extra cost savings of $150,000 to the company.
- Recruited, trained, and developed a staff of over thirty people from scratch.
- Upgraded the computer installation from an IBM 370/145 to an IBM 370/155. Later upgraded to a multi-CPU environment by adding an IBM 370/158.
- With no impact on the user community, moved the data center into a new building on two consecutive weekends.
- Recommended a tape library management system that reduced staff and saved the company $50,000 a year.

COMPUTER SYSTEMS, INC.   1973 to 1974

Shift Supervisor, Computer Operations

Duties included the supervision of the production output and quality control of Environmental Protection Agency work generated from an IBM 370/158 and 370/155 processing under V.S. II, O.S. MVT, HASP, RJE, TSO, TCAM, and Milten/Wylbur teleprocessing system. Responsible for the hiring and performance evaluation of my staff.

From 1968 to 1973 held various technical/production related jobs.

GOVERNMENT INSURANCE COMPANY   1971 to 1973

COMPUTING AND SOFTWARE, INC.   1968 to 1971

William N. Beetles   Page 3

EDUCATION

University of Miami (Florida)   1962 to 1963
   32 Credits (Business Courses)

IBM Management and Technical Seminars

PROFESSIONAL ACTIVITIES

Member—Data Processing Management Association
Member—AMDAHL Users Group

MILITARY SERVICE

U.S. Army from 1963 to 1968
Security Clearance: Top Secret Crypto

PERSONAL

Health: Excellent
Date of Birth: August 27, 1944
Hobbies: Photography, chess, and all forms of sports

Employment Objective

This typical chronological résumé starts with an objective. At
one time, all résumés began with objectives; while we feel
that this is no longer necessary we do agree that, in many
cases, an objective remains the best introduction to a résumé.
The first question most résumé-readers ask is, "What is this
person looking for?" A good way to answer this is to set forth
a clear employment goal:

- Chief executive officer of a small manufacturing com-
  pany.
- Senior operating officer in a petrochemical-oriented
  company.
- Product manager with a pharmaceutical organization.
- Manager of personnel for a medium-sized company or
  head of compensation for a large company.
- Chief financial officer.

If you write an objective, make it as specific as you can.
If you know precisely what you want and will settle for nothing else, write down that goal. If you have two objectives,
include both, but only if they are related. If they are not

related, or if you are considering more than two job possibilities, you should either write two separate résumés or mention no objectives at all (see the second sample résumé).

Background Summary

The next piece of this résumé is a short background summary, a paragraph which offers readers a quick overview of this man's career. The writer places three important points in the first line: "over eleven years of . . . experience," "results-oriented," and "data center operations." Then he expands a bit, offering specific data to support the more general statements. Given the man's objective, his résumé will certainly be looked at by computer professionals. They will not only understand the technical shorthand, they will need the data to reach a conclusion about the man's abilities. Personnel or search-firm executives may also read the résumé, and, even if they can't tell an AMDAHL V–5 from a Ford V-8, they, too, will get a better sense of this man's expertise by seeing these particulars than by reading a phrase like "extensive hardware and software experience." Details are always more intriguing than generalities.

In two short paragraphs, this résumé-writer has drawn a surprisingly detailed sketch of his career and described what he wants in his next job and what he has done to deserve it. This access speed is a basic ingredient of effective résumés. If you give a reader the chance to stop reading, he will. You need to pull him along by being clear, concise, and detailed. If you make him mutter, "Get to the point," he probably won't.

Business Experience

Next comes the body of the résumé, a detailed description of the man's business experience. Sensibly enough, he begins with his most recent place of employment, but we still see résumés that lead with an individual's first job. We wonder how many résumés have been tossed away by readers who wondered how someone could list "senior vice president—marketing" as an objective when the most prominent job on the résumé is "assistant account executive."

Some people fall into a related trap by putting their second-to-last job first. This raises crimson flags among the ranks of résumé-readers. They assume that something terrible must have happened at the most recent job. If you simply cannot emphasize your previous job, consider a functional résumé.

This sample résumé follows a standard pattern, listing company names first and then adding job titles and dates of employment. Résumés can, of course, be tailored differently. If you've held high positions at small companies, you may wish to stress titles and then name employers. If you think that the company's identity pulls more weight than your job title, put the firm's name on top. It goes without saying that, once you choose a pattern, you should stick to it throughout the résumé.

The writer of this résumé describes the responsibilities he was given at each company in short paragraphs and then lists the accomplishments he recorded in a series of short phrases. This is a good stylistic device which separates achievements from responsibilities by emphasizing both sets of information visually as well as textually.

This writer has chosen his accomplishments well. Each has a definite result which, where possible, is quantified. In his background summary, the man called himself "results-oriented." These accomplishments support that assertion.

Notice that the man doesn't list everything he's done during his career. The farther back he goes in his employment history, the less specific he becomes until, when he discusses his earliest jobs, he simply names the companies. Potential employers are normally interested in recent, major accomplishments, so there is rarely a need to go into detail about early, junior positions, unless, of course, you worked miracles at them. As it stands, this résumé describes a career marked by orderly growth and increasing responsibility.

Other Information

On the final page, the writer mentions his education and touches on other personal information. We believe that this data should be kept to a minimum. Describe your education and include management or technical seminars that you have attended. List memberships in organizations that relate to your field of work. If you think something you've done outside your career is a real asset, mention it. This man lists his service record. Normally, we might consider the information extraneous, but in this case, it is possible that the special security clearance might help the man's cause in certain industries.

But we would probably suggest to this man that he leave his hobbies off his résumé. Few employers will care whether he plays chess or takes pictures. In addition, listing too many outside activities may bring negative results: A would-be employer might wonder whether the individual will find enough spare time to do his work. In recent years, many corporate chairmen have reported that they are trying to cut back on activities that are not strictly job-related. You might follow their lead on your résumé. If you do hold an important post in some group, go ahead and mention it. Just don't let anyone get the idea that you spend your days planning what you'll do when you leave work.

In general, the simpler you keep things, the more effective your résumé becomes. But you can face Catch-22 situations. The phrase, "Health: Excellent," is most often thoroughly meaningless on a résumé, but, if you omit it, someone may think, "Maybe he's not in such good health." Or, since it is against the law to consider age when hiring someone, you shouldn't have to include it. But if you don't, someone might ask, "Just how old is this guy?" It's probably best to include both pieces of information. But consider your own needs. If you are 63 years old and ready for a new business challenge, don't list your age. Wait for a face-to-face encounter to dispel stereotypes and replace them with an exhibition of your experience and energy.

Finally, consider the things that are not included in this résumé. There is no mention of references. Don't give out names until there is a real need to do so. You don't want your references bothered until you are being considered for a specific job.

There are also no details about salary. It is too early to offer unsolicited details on that subject. If you discuss pay now, you may knock yourself out of contention for jobs later on. Suppose you write a low salary figure in your résumé. A potential employer may conclude that you cannot possibly have enough experience to handle a higher-paid job that he wants to fill. If you quote a high salary, on the other hand, someone could decide—without asking you—that you wouldn't be interested in a job that pays somewhat less. You should be the only one to reach that decision. If something doesn't serve a real need in a résumé, it shouldn't be there.

Other Examples

Look at the second sample résumé, which also follows the chronological format. Its writer didn't include a job objective, a decision that would no doubt horrify traditionalists who argue that résumés lacking objectives bewilder or irritate readers. We disagree. If, as we mentioned earlier, you know exactly what you want to do, you should announce that fact with an objective. But if you think that you might be willing to consider a variety of possibilities, writing down an objective could limit the scope of your search unnecessarily.

This writer opens his résumé with a short summary, a few lines that give a general picture of his business experience. When a potential employer reads the summary, he could read things into it, fitting its writer's abilities to the company's needs.

Dana Maitland
455 Glen Oak Drive
New Hyde Park, LI
Home: (203) 555-1234
Office: (203) 555-3498

SUMMARY:

—Profit and loss responsibility for $80-million-plus diversified
international division

—Held increasingly responsible senior financial positions in
units generating sales of $50 to $700 million annually

—Under Chief Operating Officer of a $2.4-billion company,
served as head of task force on consolidations and
divestments.

EMPLOYMENT HISTORY:

1960–Present	THE WHITE HALL COMPANY
1977–Present	*Vice President*/Products Manufactured For Consumer

$700-million group engaged in
marketing and manufacturing of
consumer and industrial products:
—Coordinated planning and analysis
of consolidation of two major
operating divisions resulting in $2.5-
million savings.
—Directed planning of the formation
of new division consolidating
vacuum cleaner and power tool
businesses resulting in
administrative savings of $1 million
and curtailment of capital spending
of $3 million.

1975–1977   *Office of the Chairman*

On special assignment to the Chairman and Chief Operating Officer, headed up consolidations and divestment projects:
—Responsible for directing the consolidation of two divisions into one major entity of $1.2 billion. Eliminated duplicate administrative costs saving $7 million over two years.
—Analyzed, recommended, and implemented the disposal of a $25-million unprofitable furniture business located in France.
—Directed the disposal of a $15-million knitting machine business in North Carolina.

Dana Maitland   Page 2

1973–1975   *Vice President—General Manager/* Special Products Division

Profit and loss responsibility for $80-million division:
—Converted a $15-million unprofitable vacuum cleaner business to a $40-million profitable business by cost reduction, change in pricing policy and customer base.
—Directed a major profit-improvement and asset-reduction program to substantially reduce losses of a $65-million appliance business located in Italy.
—Negotiated a supply agreement with a Japanese manufacturer for

knitting machines, avoiding a $12-
million investment.
—Directed the development of a new
line of sewing cabinets, resulting in
improved sales in excess of 10%.

1972–1973   *Vice President of Operations/*
Industrial Products Group

A $500-million international group
engaged in manufacturing and
marketing of industrial and consumer
products:
—Reviewed and evaluated divisional
operating performance against plans
on a continuing basis.
—Instituted profit improvement
programs to insure continued profit
performance.

1968–1972   *Vice President & Group Controller/*
Industrial Products Group

—Participated in evaluation and
recommendation of acquisition of
$10-million air conditioning
business which.is presently at $50
million.
—Developed early warning technique
to insure attainment of financial
plans.
—Developed method of analyzing
budget changes to assist non-
financial executives in evaluation of
budgets.
—Participated in the divestment of
$100 million of unprofitable
businesses.

1960–1968   *Controllership*—Divisional and Plant
Levels

1959–1960	STROMDAY, INC., Weston Instruments Division
	Assistant Controller
1956–1959	ELECTRIC GENERAL CORP., Air Conditioning Division
	Cost Accountant

EDUCATION/PERSONAL:

B.S., Accounting—Rutgers University
Date of Birth: December 29, 1930

Here are some additional examples of good summary statements:

- More than 21 years of progressive experience in the manufacture of precision mechanical and electronic instrumentation. A broad and highly successful record in the introduction of new products and cost control programs. Strong background in organization and human development in a fast-growing company.

- A seasoned general manager with a 27-year record of problem solving and profit management:

  Successful at all levels of retail marketing management, from store manager to full profit responsibility for an 80-store chain.

  A proven record in wholesale marketing from territory salesman to the general management of a $60-million profit center.

  Gained insight into the "people" side of business by managing personnel (including labor relations) for a major corporation.

  Participative management style which requires involvement with business problems. Energetic, creative, and profit-oriented.

Twenty years of experience in the retail industry. Major strengths are in staff merchandising and marketing operations.

Outstanding record of developing merchandising/promotion programs that result in number-one position. Substantial experience in store operations, accomplishing profit goals through department managers.

If you decide to start your own résumé with a summary, find the points that should be stressed by looking back through your lists of skills and accomplishments. Make sure that everything you include in the summary is supported by precise accomplishments in the body of your résumé, however. If your summary makes you sound like the hero of modern business, but your accomplishments are somewhat less than heroic, guess which items will be used to measure you.

Here, in another good example of a chronological format, an individual shows that you don't need the experience of a captain of industry to create a good résumé:

CHRONOLOGICAL FORMAT

TRACY JOHNSON
14 Middletown Road
Winthrop, Connecticut 51506
(203) 555-9876

OBJECTIVE: An administrative position offering responsibility and opportunity for advancement to management level.

EXPERIENCE:

4/76–PRESENT

XYZ CORPORATION *Administrative Assistant to Vice President, Marketing*

Prepared résumés and mailings (both Company and Executive Search Firms) for terminated executives as part of our Outplacement Counseling Program (OPC).

Monitored Mag Card Operation dealing with OPC mailings as well as special projects.

Coordinated special projects (i.e. training seminars, OPC presentations, and workshops).

10/73–3/76

SIMON & SCHUSTER *Administrative Assistant to Vice President, Director of Marketing (10/73–9/75)*

Arranged editorial meetings and coordinated activities of Sales Promotion-Advertising, Art, Publicity and Rack Departments, working as liaison between my boss and heads of these departments.

Researched *Times Sunday Book Review* and *Publishers Weekly* for articles on our books, kept record of competition ratings and a daily sales record on status of current best sellers, maintaining daily record of upcoming publication schedule as much as six months in advance.

Handled correspondence for and with various authors.

Helped organize author's parties for upcoming books and worked with motion picture companies for movie/T.V. tie-ins.

Personal Secretary to Vice President, Treasurer (9/75–3/76)

Scheduled meetings, appointments and handled correspondence.

Kept log of bids from various real estate people, furniture salesman, etc., in preparation for relocation of offices.

Typed financial budgets, quarterly reports, and prepared special reports to Gulf-Western.

Tracy Johnson   Page 2

9/72–7/73

QUINDATA   *Marketing Service Representative*

Demonstrated automatic typewriters (both cassette and paper tape) for salesmen and potential customers and conducted special seminars in the office.

Instructed people how to operate the machine after the sale was made and, working closely with the salesman to learn the customer's requirements, then programmed and prepared a customized manual specifically demonstrating these applications.

Made periodic visits to all accounts to check on their progress with the machine, answering questions and/or solving problems as they arose, either by phone or in person.

When not visiting accounts, managed the office, logged service calls as well as helped solicit for new accounts, and attended seminars to become familiar with new equipment and learn the competition's machines.

6/67–6/72

AMERICAN PRESIDENT LINES   *Girl Friday (6/67–9/68)*

Engineering Department

Typed specifications, drydock reports, bids, and computed bids from various shiprigging vendors.

Offshore Personnel Department

Assisted seamen in filling out their papers (off duty, shore level, vacation), typing and filing same in the office. Kept a running record with our home office in San Francisco and all our other port offices via teletype, notifying them of personnel requests, receiving and filling out requests from them as well. Typed and computed pay vouchers.

Claims

Typed Seamen's compensation forms and claims for lost and damaged cargo. Typed correspondence and attended claims investigations and recorded same.

Port Captain's Office

Teletyped daily ship's status report (all ship's movements).

Tracy Johnson   Page 3

EDUCATION:

New York University	Associate Degree in Applied Sciences (Business to be completed in 1983).
	Administrative Assistant Certificate Course (typing, shorthand, communications).
New School for Social Research	Various liberal arts courses taken during summer months for my own personal enjoyment.

Terry Bates, who created the fourth sample résumé, used the functional style well, organizing her accomplishments to back up the claims she made in her summary.

FUNCTIONAL FORMAT

TERRY P. BATES

29 Stonewall Lane   Home: (202) 555-4920
Washington, D.C. 87053   Office: (202) 555-7000

SUMMARY

Over 19 years of increasing responsibilities in areas of Project Management, Strategic and Short Range Planning, MIS, New Product Planning, and Operations/Budget Controls.

MAJOR ACCOMPLISHMENTS

Strategic Planning

Structured MBO programs resulting in elimination or reduction of several low-priority programs and intensification of effort for three highly promising program leads.

Working closely with senior management, developed standards and implemented MIS to monitor and analyze long- and short-range plan performance.

Modeled a new product "success grid" which highlighted the organization's inability to meet long-range goals; this led to an intensified license and acquisition program.

Identified long-range space/manpower limitations resulting in the construction of a new $2.1 million building to house needed increase of technical staff.

As a member of a four-member Systems Review Board, played an instrumental role in establishing and implementing divisional long-range systems strategy. Several duplicate projects were eliminated and investment returns optimized through priority allocations of capital and MIS budgets.

Information Systems

Directed the development of an automated resource/ priority-based planning and control system for a multimillion dollar world-wide operation. This system provided realistic scheduling, identification of manpower/ facilities bottlenecks and served as a basis for tactical decisions.

Developed a departmental MIS which surfaced inefficient use of limited resources, thus avoiding $1,500,000 of non-contributory expense.

Directed the development of an automated regulatory tracking system which improved, by five fold, compliance with governmental agency requests for research information.

Created a manpower deployment information system which formed the basis for eliminating unprofitable programs as well as intensifying priority projects.

Worked with software companies evaluating and customizing commercially available programs for specialized applications avoiding the necessity of in-house development of major systems.

Terry P. Bates   Page 2

New Product Planning

Assumed responsibility for the planning and control of more than 200 new product projects; several representing investments of up to $15,000,000.

Steered an extremely important new product to regulatory submission on time and with maximized quality, avoiding a potential $20,000,000 loss in sales.

Formed eight project-coordinating teams of multidiscipline functions, resulting in improved quality and timeliness of technical programs.

Established information exchange procedures with

licensed and joint venture participants which
insured compliance with the terms of the arrangements.

Operations/Budget Controls

Responsible for a $500,000 departmental budget with up
to twenty professional employees.

Made recommendations on "risk spending" investments
which increased new product sales potentials by
approximately $65,000,000.

Designed and implemented new product budget controls
providing readily available cost information for variance
analyses as well as documentation to support joint
venture allocation expenses.

Established and controlled critical material-allocation
plans for new chemical agents which optimized effective
utilization of limited supplies.

WORK EXPERIENCE

1968–Present	*Henry Morris Corporation*
	1977 Director, Operations Planning
	1975 Associate Director, Projects Planning
	1973 Manager, New Product Planning
	1968 New Product Coordinator
1964–1968	*Seldon Products, Inc.*
	Assistant Director, Product Development
1961–1964	*Merrimack Products, Inc.*
	Assistant Pilot Plant Supervisor.

M.B.A.	(Executive Program), Fairleigh Dickinson University. 1976
B.S.	(Chemistry) Brooklyn College. 1960

Age:	39 years
Health:	Excellent

This résumé also illustrates a structural element that is both an important component of all good résumés and an area in which functional résumés can be particularly effective: It touches all pertinent bases. You not only need to back up what you say, you also need to demonstrate that you have experience in the main areas of responsibility that the kind of job you are looking for demands. Without even reading this résumé, a potential employer could glance at it and learn that the woman it describes has had extensive experience in four major business areas. In addition, if a reader were interested in this individual's achievements in one specific functional area, he wouldn't have to sift through separate job descriptions to search for relevant details.

The next résumé also follows the functional style, although, in this instance, employment history precedes accomplishments. But the emphasis is still on functional areas of accomplishments, not on dates or companies.

Notice how the writer compresses a twenty-year career into a few pages without giving the impression that he has loafed through the last two decades. Try to limit your own résumé to two typewritten pages. If you have had a great deal of exceptional experience, you may expand the document to a third or fourth page. But make sure that everything you write down earns its place. Don't make a reader wade through repetitive or extraneous material. Don't assume that a long résumé is the same as a good résumé.

FRANCIS M. HUMPHREY
22 Butternut Drive
Springfield, OH 44090
(603) 555-6144

OBJECTIVES

Profit Center Accountability
Corporate, Commercial, or Market Development

SUMMARY

Over twenty years technical, marketing, corporate
management experience with specialty industrial products.
Includes product development, marketing, plant management,
technology commercialization, new ventures, planning,
acquisitions, and divestitures.

BUSINESS AFFILIATIONS

LUCITE CORPORATION (Adhesives & Sealants)	Division Manager	1976–Present
	Market Development Manager	1961–1970
VEENER INDUSTRIES (Controls, Fasteners, Plastics)	Manager-Corporate Development	1972–19753
ENSIGN-BICKWORTH (Chemical Specialties)	Consultant (on retainer)	1971
W.S. WRENCH COMPANY (Metal Stamping Machinery)	Assistant Sales Manager	1958–1961
ELASTIC NUT CORP. (Specialty Fasteners)	Manager Technical Service	1956–1958
DART AERONAUTICAL (Aircraft Engines)	Project Engineer	1951–1955

MAJOR ACCOMPLISHMENTS

Corporate Development

Established function at Veener under CEO. Set division criteria. Acquired four companies adding $10MM in sales. Organized divestiture of $5MM misfit division. Assessed external opportunities for Lucite. Performed acquisition research.

Planned strategically for growth in sales, EPS, ROI. Conducted business analyses of key industries including electronics, industrial controls, fasteners, adhesives and sealants, plastics, fluid power, electrical products.

Started engineered plastics group. Acquired $4MM leader in extruded Nylon and Delrin mill shapes. Launched precision custom molding at control products division. Negotiated with other specialty plastic converters.

Organized new Ford Motor Co.-Lucite joint venture company to sell adhesives to automotive industry. Canceled to pursue more independent and profitable line.

Operations Management

Served as General Manager of Lucite Corporation tax-exempt Puerto Rican manufacturing division for two years. Double production. Generated 1/3 of consolidated corporate earnings.

Started R&D function staffed by Puerto Rican professionals to develop proprietary adhesive monomers. Also increased process yields 20%.

Commercialization

Developed anerobic gasketing, retaining adhesives technology for machinery assembly. Published ASME papers. In 1979 product sales $15MM-plus worldwide.

Commercialized casting/weld porosity sealing technology. Matured into impregnation product line and systems profit center with $3MM sales.

Started Lucite adhesive application equipment group. Developed special devices and systems to dispense difficult liquids. Produced $10MM annual adhesive sales.

Marketing

Managed product and market managers in mixed matrix support of six profit centers delivering $40MM Lucite and Permatex line sales. Generated new product and market programs worth $3MM in sales during '78 and '79.

Segmented markets for Lucite adhesives by SIC. Researched and developed profiles by industry including automotive, electronic, medical disposables, fluid power, aerospace, etc. Developed $4MM sales.

Organized random adhesive applications into patterns via data bank. Developed "job identified" application-oriented products for fasteners, fittings, bushings, seals, bearings, etc. Expanded bearing distributor sales $15MM in six years.

Administered staff of application and technical service engineers supporting 120 salesmen selling Lucite and Permatex industrial brands. Organized nationwide technical center decentralization to improve heavy phone, lab, field service, and technical training. Produced product-performance information.

PROFESSIONAL PROFILE

B.S., M.E.—Lehigh U.—1951
Business Management—RPI—1966
Management—Amos Tuck—1979
AMA—Marketing, new products, acquisition
Member—ASME, SAE, Assoc. Corporate Growth
ASME Technical papers: Two patents

PERSONAL DATA

U.S. Citizen

Health—Excellent

The key to brevity is to write a draft résumé and then mercilessly pare away *everything* that does not absolutely have to be included. If you can think of one word that will take the place of two others, use it. Short words are often stronger than long words, and they take up less space. Use them. Check your grammar and spelling. This editing process can transform a meandering four-page résumé into a tight, action-oriented gem. Here is a final example of a functional résumé which is short and to the point, a simple and effective description of the writer's work history.

FUNCTIONAL FORMAT

JEAN C. SAMUELSON
1432 Ninth Avenue
Louisville, Kentucky 65432
(502) 555-1792

SUMMARY

Twelve years of broad-based experience in the insurance industry, encompassing supervision, training, and the performance of detail analysis, review, and reconciliation of listings and contract reports.

EXPERIENCE:

	ABC Life Insurance Company, 1966–1978
1977–1978	*Dividend Specialist* (Team leader of five employees)
1974–1977	*Senior Analyst* (Team leader of three employees)
1966–1974	*Figure Clerk* (Calculating interest rates, check for accuracy, proofing)

Coordinated the release of both checks ($10,000 to $2,000,000) and contract reports after verifying accuracy.

Devised and wrote a technical procedures manual for divisional employees, significantly reducing the number of processing errors.

Analyzed for accuracy and journalized various contract holders' reports.

Trained and supervised all new divisional employees in specific job functions (typing, dividend calculations, and filing), resulting in increased productivity.

Maintained extensive contact with group representative regarding requests for contract changes and information.

Reconciled errors in detail listings (reserve funds, dividends, expenses) to correct oversights.

Assigned priority to daily work of staff, to insure both orderly work flow and completion on a timely basis.

Maintained high staff morale by establishing a team-approach environment.

Prepared quarterly dividend reports to reconcile ABC's financial statements with client's reports.

Jean Samuelson   Page 2

EDUCATION

N.Y.C.C.C.   49 credits in Accounting

Short Courses:

Keypunch machine school
Effective Report and Letter Writing
Career Development Seminars
(Women and Minorities)

OUTSIDE INTERESTS

Bowling & Cooking

Unless you have access to an excellent typewriter, it's worthwhile to have your résumé typed professionally so that you can make copies from a crisp original. You will need 500 copies, so usually the best course is to have them offset. You may, however, decide to use a copying machine for the first fifty or so, just in case an early reader spots a glaring error. If you use a copying machine, make sure that it produces strong, clean copies. Don't hand out résumés that are faint and shadowy or dark and smudged. Make it apparent that you took the time to produce your résumé properly. For reading ease, choose ivory, beige, or even soft pastel paper (*very* soft . . . avoid lime green).

Don't make your résumé look *too* slick, however. Don't have it typeset, for instance. You don't want anyone to conclude that you needed professional help, particularly since you've taken the time to do the job yourself. Don't put a photograph on your résumé. Keep things simple. Don't let your résumé get in your way.

6 * Marketing Strategy

You're ready to go public now. It's time to arrange interviews that will lead to firm job offers. To do this, you will need to develop a marketing strategy—tactics and priorities that determine the search activities you will pursue and the emphasis each will receive.

Our clients use four techniques to find new jobs.

- *Personal contacts* account for 70% of the positions they take.
- *Executive search firms or placement agencies* lead them to 15% of their new jobs.
- *Direct mailings* produce 10%.
- *Published openings* account for 5%.

The key to a successful marketing strategy is to touch all bases by pursuing *each* search avenue. The fact that personal contacts produce seven of every ten new jobs for our clients does not mean that you should devote all your time to this tactic. Remember that 30% of these new jobs come from other sources. You only need one job; don't limit your horizons by arbitrarily excluding yourself from any legitimate search technique.

But do not devote too much time to tactics that obviously don't deserve the effort. Many people, for instance, feel uncomfortable asking for favors or approaching relative strangers for assistance. Typically, they resist building personal contact networks and retreat to what they think is safer ground, spending most of their time answering advertisements or mailing out résumés. They avoid the face-to-face contact that worries them, but they also insulate themselves from most job opportunities.

Let the search technique's effectiveness determine the amount of time you devote to it. Assume that you will spend thirty-five hours a week actually working at your search. Based on our clients' experiences, we think that you should devote, on average, 70% of that time—about twenty-five hours—to creating and expanding a network of personal contacts. Spend about five hours working with search firms or employment agencies. Take three or four hours to create a direct mailing to targeted companies. Answer help-wanted advertisements for an hour or two each week.

Your own schedule may need fine-tuning. If you don't have substantial business experience, for example, you may find that, at first, you don't have enough contacts to spend 70% of your week building a network. Should that occur, you can devote relatively more hours to other tactics—answering ads or contacting employment agencies, for instance—until the expansion that is a natural part of the networking process makes it possible for you to spend more time developing these critical contacts.

If you are looking for—and deserve—a position high on the job pyramid, something in the six-figure salary range, then you will probably find it useful to spend more than 15% of your time working with leading executive search firms. They concentrate on this end of the employment spectrum.

Or, if you have decided to make a radical career change, you may discover that the skills and accomplishments described in your résumé don't quite meet the qualifications of the jobs that really interest you. Since you won't match their expectations exactly, there is a greater than normal likelihood that résumé readers will screen you out before you get a chance to explain your new goals. In such a situation, we suggest that you devote proportionally more time to the face-to-face encounters that typify the networking process. During these meetings, you'll get a chance to articulate your plans and sell your abilities in a manner that simply can't be accomplished in a résumé.

But in general, don't give away any options. You need to generate as many interviews as you can: It takes an average of eight to land one job offer. Ideally, you should have two or even three offers to consider when it comes time to make a final decision about your next job. If you end your job search enjoying this embarrassment of riches—and the situation really does occur—it will probably be a result of having set up sixteen to twenty-four employment interviews along the way.

Published Openings

Answering help-wanted advertisements is a time-honored and, many insist, singularly ineffective way to find a job. It is true that only 5% of the jobs our clients accept come from this process. But it is also true that these ads make 5% of our clients 100% employed.

If you rely exclusively on the employment sections of newspapers and trade publications, you'll certainly have put all your eggs into a very flimsy basket. But if you think of the process as one part of your search, you may be pleasantly surprised. People really do find their jobs through the *New York Times,* the *Houston Post, Advertising Age, Chemical Week,* or any of a number of other consumer and publisher publications.

Responding to an ad can seem like dropping your résumé into a bottomless pit, of course, particularly when the ad is identified only with a box number. Many of these ads do not describe real jobs. Search firms place them to build files of résumés in particular fields. Other agencies try to drum up business by approaching major employers with unsolicited mailings of stacks of résumés. To keep this scattershot maneuver going, they obviously need to replenish their stock of résumés constantly. Companies may decide to test the employment waters by placing ads to determine talent availability and salary level for specific jobs. Blind ads become relatively inexpensive research tools for them.

But box-number advertisements can also describe real job opportunities. The hiring company may wish to remove someone from its staff without telegraphing the decision until a successor has been located. Or a would-be employer may simply want to protect himself from having to acknowledge the hundreds of inquiries that a single ad can produce.

In general, if the company does name itself, you can expect to receive at least a form letter thanking you for your interest. You may not get this response for several months, but most companies think that a polite thank-you note is a cheap form of good public relations. Other companies, however, include this sentence in their ads: "Only individuals selected for further consideration will be contacted." Don't haunt your mailbox waiting for news about ads you have answered.

Since there is no infallible way to determine the legitimacy of an ad, we think that you should go ahead and answer any that seem interesting to you. There is little to lose and, potentially, a great deal to gain by taking a few minutes to send off a résumé and short cover letter.

Even when advertisements describe legitimate job openings, however, the odds of getting past the initial screening process remain low. A single ad may draw 400 to 500 responses, and even the most conscientious résumé-reader may succumb to a case of glazed eyes by the time he or she reaches number 302. If that is your résumé, it may not get the attention it deserves.

Responses are usually put into one of three categories. The first group contains excellent possibilities, résumés of individuals who appear to meet or surpass the job's predetermined specifications. The second group holds the résumés of possible choices, people who probably meet the job requirements but who, for one reason or another (which may be subjective), don't seem quite as qualified as members of the first group. Résumés that land in the third category come from people who do not seem qualified for the position. They are likely to be discarded. Your objective is to see to it that your response lands in one of the first two piles.

While your résumé is probably not a perfect match for any advertisement, you can write a good cover letter to tie your résumé to the job you are investigating. When you locate an ad that interests you, study it to isolate three or four key requirements of objectives that it stresses. Mention each qualification in your cover letter, tailoring a skill or accomplishment from your résumé to the specific job. Even if you have stressed the key items in your résumé, restate them in the cover letter. Help the reader simplify the screening process by making it unnecessary for him to dig into your résumé to determine whether you fit his specifications. A good cover note will convince him that you do.

Consider this advertisement as an example:

REGIONAL SALES MANAGER

Leading plastics manufacturer seeks successful sales executive to head its $7-million Southwest region. Ideal candidate will be a results-oriented achiever with an impressive track record in industrial plastic sales and at least four years of successful sales supervision. Must have demonstrated training ability. Position requires approximately 40% travel. Send résumé with salary requirements.

Here, the key requirements appear to be:
- track record in industrial plastic sales
- four years of sales supervision
- demonstrated training ability

You should refer to each in your cover letter, and you should also consider the tone of the ad when you respond.

Such words as "successful," "results-oriented," "achiever," and "impressive" tell you how to answer the ad. Your cover letter might begin:

> As the attached résumé indicates, I am a successful sales manager whose commitment to bottom-line results has been demonstrated during eight years of aggressive sales experience with Lucid, Inc., a $15-million manufacturer of industrial plastic products. For the past five years, I have supervised a nine-member sales staff and managed the company's sales training programs. Last year, my staff and I increased sales by 14% over the previous year.

Respond to both the substance and the tone of the ad. You can almost play it back to the people who devised it.

Don't pre-screen yourself. If, to continue with the example above, you have had only three years of sales management experience, go ahead and answer the ad, but don't mention the three-year figure in your cover letter. Or, if the job really interests you, don't exclude yourself from the competition because you're not sure that you're as fast-track or results-oriented a candidate as the company seems to be looking for. If everyone were as aggressive as personnel-ad writers apparently want them to be, newspaper employment sections would have to be printed on stainless steel pages. Since it is currently a popular management trait, many employers like to think that they are hyperaggressive when, really, they are not. Once the talk stops and the decision-making begins, they hire people they feel comfortable with.

You want the company to get in touch with you. If it does, you'll have plenty of time to decide whether its style matches your own, and you'll have much better evidence to work from than a single advertisement. If, however, an ad identifies the company, and you know from experience that it is simply *not* the kind of organization you want to work for, then don't send off a résumé. You're not looking for just any job. You're interested in the right job.

Our sample ad asks for "salary requirements." In most cases, we advise our clients not to mention money, even if salary information is requested. Salary level is often used as a screening device, and it can knock you out of the game before you get a chance to sit down for an interview with the company. If your credentials look right, you will probably interest a prospective employer even if you haven't said how much you make or would like to make. But if your skills seem appropriate and you set a salary level somewhat above the company's limit, you could be dismissed from further consideration. In a face-to-face interview, however, you might convince the employer that you're actually worth the amount you seek. Or you might envision such a good future with the company that you would decide to moderate your immediate salary demands.

If your salary history or requirements seem too low, a company could conclude that you don't have enough experience to handle the job. Worse still, someone might assume that you've lied about your qualifications.

There are a few situations in which you should mention salary. You might decide to do some screening of your own, for example. If you're looking for $100,000 a year and will not consider anything less, you might mention that fact in your cover letter. But understand that this will limit the number of responses substantially. Finally, if a company is so determined to learn your salary that its ad includes the line, "Inquiries without salary information will not be considered," you'll most likely have to mention a figure to stand any chance of getting a response.

Generally speaking, however, don't offer a salary figure unless one is demanded in no uncertain terms. But don't let anyone think you left it out because you didn't read the ad. In your cover letter, include a sentence like, "Before providing a meaningful and sensible salary figure, I will have to discuss the responsibilities and opportunities presented by this job in somewhat greater detail."

When you finish a cover letter, think for a moment before you clip it to your résumé and mail both away. Even with today's sporadic mail service, the bulk of the responses to an ad hit the recruiter's desk two or three days after the ad has run. One way to avoid being on the bottom of the pile is to wait a day or two (but not much longer) before sending in your materials. You résumé will land on a somewhat cleaner desk, where it will stand a better chance of getting a thorough reading.

If you haven't heard anything at the end of two weeks, but feel strongly that the job may really be made for you, write again, emphasizing the fact that, because the job seems so suited to your needs and abilities, you thought that you should at least send along another résumé. You may discover that your first résumé never reached its destination, or that it disappeared as it was being handed from one company official to another. Take nothing for granted.

If someone's name is included in the advertisement, you might give him a call. If the ad states, "No calls, please," wait a couple of weeks before phoning. Tell the individual that although your résumé apparently didn't meet the requirements of the advertised position, you remain interested in the company and would like to arrange a short meeting to discuss the firm. Our experience has been that company representatives respond very positively to this sort of interest and energy.

In one instance, a man we counseled answered a newspaper ad for a job that he thought was totally in line with his career goals. Two weeks passed and no word came back to him. Even though he realized that the ad could have been placed by someone stockpiling résumés, it interested him so greatly that he sent off another résumé and a second cover letter. He got a telephone call a few days later and learned that one of the screening criteria for the job was a test of persistence. Only people who responded twice were considered for the position. Our client went in for an interview and landed the job which, interestingly enough, was a counseling position with a church.

Company Mailings

When you considered your skills, needs, and employment goals during the planning and organizing phase of your job search, you created a relatively precise picture of an ideal job or, perhaps, of several interesting career possibilities. One way to contact the companies and organizations that survive this winnowing process is to create a direct mail package—a cover letter and résumé or a single document combining the two—and send it to an appropriate individual at each targeted firm.

Our clients normally mail these packages to at least 100 companies. Typically, they receive two or three solid invitations to employment interviews as a result. These interviews, in turn, lead to 10% of the jobs that our clients accept as they resume their careers.

There is no escaping the fact that distributing a company mailing, like answering a want-ad, is a low-yield endeavor. But if you are determined to take the time to find the right job for yourself, you shouldn't throw away opportunities that, 10% of the time, have found other people their right jobs. Don't assume that you are wasting time by pursuing this tactic.

The cover letter that accompanies your résumé in a mailing should be short, informal, and persuasive. Try to emphasize quickly—and in an interesting manner—who you are and what you have to offer. If there is something unique about your background or abilities, mention it. Don't restate your résumé; you are going to send it along, too. Try to raise a few highlights that will attract a reader's interest. Be sure to tell the person you are writing how he or she can contact you. You may also indicate that you will follow up your letter with a telephone call. If you do include this line, however, be sure to actually make that call.

COMPANY LETTER

John C. Sloan
32 Center Street
Northport, California 90000

Mr. Amos Tucker
Senior Vice President
Mid Central Industries
Wichita, Kansas

Dear Mr. Tucker:

I am an international executive of a major company, with general management experience (headquarters and overseas) and a strong marketing background.

Recently, I proposed and carried out the decentralization of our _____, which I managed for the past two years. In effect, this action eliminated my own position as Director and General Manager. Because the alternative positions offered to me are out of line with my career goals, I have decided to seek employment elsewhere, and my management is aware of this decision.

My objective is to obtain a senior line or staff management position, preferably in a multi-national firm, and I am willing to relocate.

If my résumé matches any of your current openings, I would be pleased to meet with you. I'll call you in a few days to see if you're interested in setting up an interview. You can call me at (333) 555-1111.

Sincerely,

/cu
Enclosure   John C. Sloan

Anthony Bracer
3 Owens Road
Midland, Ohio 54321

Mr. C. James Cavelli
Director of Personnel
Insatco Ltd.
Dover, Delaware 12345

Dear Mr. Cavelli:

I recently mentioned to John Jones, a friend at Simpson
Industries, that I do not find sufficient challenge in my present
position. He told me of Insatco's growth record and possible
interest in seasoned executives with international experience,
and suggested that I contact you.

Briefly, my qualifications comprise twenty years of
progressively responsible experience including six years of
"bottom line" P&L responsibility and twelve years of line and
staff marketing management. In terms of depth and diversity, I
have:

> Prepared successful marketing and business plans, both
> single- and multi-country, focusing on market
> penetration, profitability, and effective resource
> allocation.
>
> Organized and effectively staffed sales advertising,
> marketing, and general management functions.
>
> Prepared and directed successful marketing campaigns
> at foreign subsidiary and headquarters levels.
>
> Assessed and negotiated acquisition, licensing, and joint
> venture agreements.

I would very much appreciate an exploratory meeting to
determine how my qualifications might match some of your

current or planned management needs, in either the domestic or international areas. I will call you to see if we can arrange such an interview. I can be reached at (222) 555-1234.

Sincerely,

/cu
Enclosure   Anthony Bracer

Look at these two sample letters. While the first is an acceptable, workmanlike note that describes the overall background of its writer, the second is clearly a superior effort. It begins with a reference—the name of an individual known to both the writer and the recipient. These two individuals have one thing in common at the outset: They both know John Jones. As we shall see when we discuss personal contact networks, this kind of reference point lowers barriers and opens doors to interviews.

The second letter also offers specific details about the career accomplishments of the individual it describes. A reader won't have to wade through a résumé to make an initial assessment of its writer. If the highlights mentioned in the letter pique the reader's interest, his natural inclination will be to turn to the résumé for additional information.

This letter also shows that the writer has done enough homework to realize that this company might be an ideal place for him to seek employment. The reader learns that the writer has taken the time to discover what he does well, what he would like to do next, and where he thinks he might do it. The writer is approaching the company from a very positive reference point: He isn't trying to shape himself to the company's needs but is demonstrating that he and the company may share similar aims. This person isn't asking, he's offering.

Marketing Letters

In the past year, some of our clients have begun to experiment with a new method of preparing company mailings. They write and distribute marketing letters, single documents that combine the strong points of cover letters and résumés in one piece of effective business correspondence.

The goal of any company mailing is to get and hold the attention of an appropriate decision-maker at the target firm in the hope that he or she will grant an interview. But since the mailing is unsolicited, this is not always an easy task. Some observers feel that sending out an unsolicited résumé only inspires its recipient to forward the material in one of two undesirable directions: to the personnel department's files or toward the wastebasket. The thinking behind a marketing letter is that it may avoid a stereotypical "I'll-scream-if-I-have-to-read-another-résumé" reaction and gives its writer a better than average chance to attract attention and get his message across. A good business letter, the argument goes, is more likely to interest someone than a good résumé.

So far, our clients have had mixed results with this technique. Some have reported remarkable success rates, landing fifteen or even twenty interviews by sending out 100 marketing letters. Others have found that the tactic did not work at all for them and fell below the typical one-to-two-percent response rate of a standard résumé and cover letter mailing.

Perhaps our sample is still too small to draw valid conclusions about the tactic. Exceptionally high rates of return may have been caused by the exceptional qualifications of a few individuals. But one thing seems clear: Marketing letters are only effective if they are particularly well-written.

If you choose to write one, you'll need to create a vigorous, hard-hitting, and energetic business letter that sells your qualifications unequivocally. You should base the letter on solid accomplishments: "I've been cutting costs for more than fifteen years, and I've saved more than $20 million in the process." There is no room for modesty or reticence in a good marketing letter.

The first paragraph of such a personal sales letter should tell what you've done and how well you've done it. Include quantifiable measurements wherever possible, numbers and percentages that can't be argued with. Then, in the body of your letter, you should expand and embellish this introduction, continuing to be as specific as you can about your achievements.

Close the letter with a quick sales pitch that indicates the action you would like a reader to take—an invitation to a discussion on the topic of how your experience might benefit his or her organization.

Think of your letter as a direct-mail advertising brochure. You are the product, and you want your audience to act by contacting you for an interview. Use the sample letters as guides for creating one of your own.

MARKETING LETTER

> Marvin S. LeBrun
> 3841 Broad Street
> San Francisco, California 99999

Ms. Nancy C. Slater
President
Food Service Incorporated
Albuquerque, New Mexico 2241

Dear Ms. Slater:

As the Regional Vice President for Westco Services, I directed the development of Northern California and the Southwest. Working from a 10-year plan, we anticipated developing thirty to fifty units and $30 million in revenues. In five years we achieved the plan by developing thirty units of coffee shops, dinner houses, and specialty theme restaurants, and $28 million in revenues. I began with 2 restaurants.

In Southern California we concentrated on developing three areas, Newport Beach, San Diego, and Riverside. These areas are directed and controlled from San Diego, utilizing the commissary cluster unit approach. Three major facets of this concept are control over the quantity and quality of the food; storage and warehousing of inventories to reduce costs to the individual units; and the reduction of suppliers to a manageable number with an increase in items supplied by them. This reduction has saved the firm $100,000 annually.

The enormous success of this approach encouraged us to utilize this same concept in Phoenix, Arizona, and Albuquerque, New Mexico. These units have also prospered. Along with the commissary in Phoenix, we have established five coffee shops, three dinner houses, and one theme restaurant. While in the Albuquerque area, we established a commissary, three coffee shops and two dinner houses.

As a result of the success of developing the Southwest, I was promoted to District Vice President of Operations. I currently have responsibility for ninety coffee shops, dinner houses, and theme restaurants located nationwide with $85 million in revenues.

My varied and proven experience in the food service industry is only briefly touched on in this letter. I would appreciate the opportunity to personally explore with you in more detail how this experience could benefit your company.

Please write to me at my residence shown above or telephone me either at my office or home.

Sincerely,

Office: (800) 555-1000
Home: (800) 555-2468   Marvin S. LeBrun

Harold Stormer
676 Archer Avenue
Miami, Florida 42733
(555) 800-1616

PERSONAL AND CONFIDENTIAL

Mr. Vance Mitchell
Chairman
The Reflex Group
Lowell, Massachusetts 12433

Dear Mr. Mitchell:

As President of Telnet, Inc., a subsidiary of Anso, Inc., $1.4 billion diversified world leader in the manufacture and distribution of electronic components, I was responsible for a $30 million division producing stereo components for the consumer products industry. In this capacity I turned the division from a loss position into black after being on the job three months. Specifically, I increased gross profit by more than 50% (over $400,000 in profit contribution). I also reduced inventories by over 100% in less than one year, a reduction of over $2 million.

Today, more than ever before, there is a strong need for leadership skills that can improve productivity, bottom-line performance, teamwork, morale, and self-motivation.

My experience also reflects an ability to cut through difficult problems and reduce them to simple common denominators. My contemporaries consider me to have a strong numbers sense providing direction in moving my company to become profitable and well-controlled.

Telnet is being moved to Korea due to high labor costs and stiff competition from foreign markets. I have decided to seek another position to challenge my skills and abilities.

Some of my other achievements are:

Developed a long-range business plan at Telnet mapping future business efforts on short- and long-term marketing strategies to meet corporate goals and objectives.

Realized savings of over $50 thousand per year by establishing a perpetual material control system which reduced costly parts shortages and waste.

In human relations, I brought together a strong and decisive management team by working with them in an open and achievement-oriented atmosphere and directing the activities of 900 people in Production, Quality Control, Marketing, Sales, Engineering, Finance, and Industrial Relations.

As Director of Operations/General Manager, increased net income by 111% during the first year on the job. During the next three years, overall net income was up by almost 200%. This resulted in savings of $2.9 million.

Instituted cost reduction programs which resulted in savings of more than $500 thousand for the past three years; among these were increased machine shop capability and computerized automatic testing capability.

Established an off-shore manufacturing facility which resulted in over $100 thousand in tax savings in one year. Future savings over the next nine years are estimated to be $1.2 million.

As Director of Finance, along with the Division President, made an acquisition that has increased sales and earnings of division by more than 25% per year.

As Controller, developed bid rates and reports for use on government D.O.D. contracts, preventing loss and lack of control on major government contracts.

Previous to my current position, I worked 11 years at a medium-sized electronics subsidiary of Stiller, Gruhewald, Inc., a $1 billion multi-national corporation. I started as Controller, progressed after five years to Director of Finance, and was again promoted after two years to Director of Operations/ General Manager of the manufacturing division.

I graduated from college with a Major in Business and was the Top Honor Graduate (GPA 4.0) in my MBA class at Pepperdine University. I am married and will relocate for a suitable position.

I would like to explore with you the contributions I can provide for your organization. Please contact me in confidence at my home.

Sincerely,

Harold Stormer

It is probably easier to write an excellent résumé and cover letter than it is to create a first-rate marketing letter. One way to determine which option you should use, as a result, is to consider your own writing skills. If you are a good writer—and particularly if you are looking for work that demands excellent writing skills—then the marketing letter is a good way to demonstrate your abilities in a direct mailing. But if you don't feel that you are a particularly good writer, then you should consider contacting target companies with a résumé and short cover letter. A badly written marketing letter may do more harm than good.

You can't expect much success from either option if your mailing doesn't get into the right person's hands. The second marketing letter sample, for instance, is stamped "Personal/Confidential." Its writer hopes that this nomenclature will keep an efficient secretary from glancing at his letter, making a unilateral decision, and consigning it to the personnel files. This tactic might work, although, to an assistant who has seen the ploy in the past, the phrase may only speed the letter to the nearest file cabinet.

The "Personal/Confidential" tag certainly won't help if it is followed by the salutation, "Dear Executive." Do your best to determine the identity of the individual who should receive your mailing at each company. This will usually be the head of your discipline at the firm.

Don't address your mailing to the director of personnel, unless, of course, you are looking for a job in that field. If you want a position as a marketing manager, for example, mail to the vice president of marketing at each firm. He may send your material right over to the personnel director, but he might attach a note saying, "This guy looks interesting. I think we should take a look at him."

If you want a job as vice president of operations, don't send a mailing to the company's vice president of operations. He's more likely to feel threatened than interested. Send it to the appropriate senior vice president or group head. If you are approaching a small company, go directly to the president or chairman.

There are several ways to find names to go with these titles. Look at the appendix at the back of this book. It lists business directories that are found in most good libraries. These books can help you determine the companies you should contact, and, in many cases, they will identify the people you should write to by name. You'll also discover telephone numbers for the companies you've targeted. A call to each firm on your target list will get you current names and addresses for your primary contacts.

If you take the time to create a mailing, make every effort to do it properly. It won't hurt to assume that if you give a reader the slightest opportunity to disregard your mailing, he or she will discard it. Every letter—whether a cover note or full-blown marketing letter—should be carefully typed and proofed. If you have taken the time to identify your contact's name, don't give away your advantage by typing it at the top of a photo-copied letter. Even the best copy looks like a copy when it is introduced by a typewritten salutation. You might contact auto-typing services or word-processing centers in your area to see whether they can create 100 typewritten letters economically for you. They'll be able to take a single letter and add a different inside address and greeting to each copy.

The key to a good direct-mail piece is to make the package look as if it has been individually prepared for each person who receives it. As simple a matter as stamping your letters rather than using a postage meter can make a real difference. All this takes time, but do it right if you do it at all.

Consider your own experience: When you receive your mail, which pieces interest you most—form letters or personal correspondence?

Executive Search Firms

Some people call them "executive search consultants," some refer to them as "flesh peddlers" and "body snatchers," and everyone else knows them as "headhunters." Whatever name they go by, executive search firms, along with the employment agencies which are generally considered to occupy a somewhat lower position in the placement business hierarchy, locate 15% of the new jobs that our clients take. Everyone has heard about these firms, but many people really don't understand how they operate or how they can be worked into a job search marketing strategy.

Many people believe that individuals go to search firms which, in turn, find jobs for them. The process actually works in just the opposite direction. Search firms work for companies, not for individuals. When a client has a position to fill, it contacts a search firm, pays the recruiter a healthy fee (usually a flat 30% to 33⅓% of the job's starting salary), and the search firm locates top candidates whose qualifications meet the specifications of the job.

Most openings are only listed with a single search company. Other search firms, no matter how reputable or well-respected they may be, usually have no involvement with a search being conducted by another recruiter. This means, of course, that individuals should contact as many search firms as they can to stand the best chance of turning up available positions.

Search firms originally existed to locate highly qualified individuals and lure them from one job to another. They only talked to people who were already employed. All that has changed, particularly since 1975, when a recession forced many capable people out of their jobs. Today, search firms understand that qualified people frequently lose jobs. The fact that 85% of our clients find new jobs at salaries equal to or better than those at their previous positions seems ample proof of this theory. So the fact that you aren't working shouldn't keep you from contacting search firms. If you have sound credentials, and if a firm is running a search that calls for these skills, its representatives will want to hear from you.

Which search organizations should you contact? We advise our clients to get in touch with 100–150 search firms. (Remember that a single job is only likely to show up at a single search firm, so you need to contact as many as you can.) The search industry includes companies of all sizes. At the top of the business are the largest search firms, the "Big Six": Korn/Ferry International, Heidrick & Struggles, Spencer Stuart & Associates, Russell Reynolds Associates, Egon Zehnder International, and Boyden Associates. Many companies are members of the Association of Executive Recruiting Consultants (AERC), an organization of about sixty leading search firms which meet certain agreed-upon standards. They are probably as good a group as any to start with. But there are many reputable search organizations that choose not to belong to AERC, so you certainly shouldn't limit yourself to its members. You can't, as a matter of fact, if you wish to get your résumé to 150 search outfits.

One variable that should enter into your choice of search firms is your salary level. The largest firms have traditionally concentrated their energies on the highest-paying jobs—those which start in the low six figures and move off into the stratosphere. Since these firms usually earn a straight percentage of the salary figure, their inclination toward the top end of the market is understandable: It's nice work if you can get it, and, generally, they can. This trend does seem to be shifting a bit, however, as search firms, which enjoy increasing their revenues as much as any company, find that there are only so many top jobs to fill.

Some of the top firms, as a result, have begun to accept search assignments well below the $100,000 level.* Many of the smaller firms have always worked in this area. As a rule of thumb, you should be looking for a salary of $50,000 or more if you hope to generate interest at most search firms. Below that level, you should spend at least some of your time investigating employment agencies. If you are near the cutoff point, go ahead and contact search firms. It's the only sure way to find out whether they are conducting searches that meet your career plans.

How do you identify and contact these search firms? If you've dealt with one in the past—either by having been contacted by a search outfit as a potential candidate for a job or by having retained a firm to locate an executive for you—you should get in touch with the consultants you've worked with. If you are a member of a professional organization, its staff may have search firm contacts. Call them and ask. As you build a personal contact network (which we'll discuss in a moment), you can ask the people you meet whether they can recommend you to search consultants. You might ask your former employer's personnel director if he has a contact at a search firm. (Don't be too proud to ask. The firm may work a little harder for you if you are referred to them by a company they are trying to impress.)

While it works to your benefit to have someone introduce you to a search firm, you can even walk into a firm's

---

* And even at firms where accepting lower-level assignments goes against official policy, there are exceptions. If, for instance, a good client which has given the firm a number of high-salary searches asks for help on a somewhat lower-paying job, it will probably be accommodated.

offices and tell the receptionist that you wish to register. You might be ushered into an immediate interview.

But to alert the greatest number of search organizations, you'll have to mail out résumés and cover letters. Don't waste any time anguishing over the style or content of your letter: Search firms work with résumés; cover letters are frequently tossed out immediately. Mention a few key points about yourself and the kind of job you are seeking. Tell how you can be reached. Ask the firm to contact you if they are handling any relevant searches and to keep your résumé on file should any pertinent assignments surface in the future.

What you don't say is probably more important than what you do mention in this type of cover letter. Don't pre-screen yourself. Don't mention the fact that you are currently unemployed, for example. It's no longer a sin with search firms, but it is still a matter that is best brought up in an interview.

You may decide to state your salary level, but not if you think it might hurt your chances with the firm. In the sample letters that follow, the salary figures seem consistent with the jobs they are linked to and are unlikely to raise eyebrows. In fact, in the second letter, mentioning the salary level is probably a very good idea. Depending on the company he or she works for, a marketing director might make from $20,000 to $120,000 a year, so a salary figure can give a search firm a good idea of the level at which an individual is equipped to work.

If, on the other hand, your salary is somewhat below the $50,000 cutoff point but you think that you are ready to step up to a position in that pay range, save the money discussion for a personal interview. Here's a good rule of thumb: When in doubt, leave it out.

The letter does not require a personal salutation and can be offset or photocopied. Of course, if you have someone's name at a particular firm, it makes sense to send a personal letter to him.

> Richard L. Jones
> 2 Barnack Way
> Jones Bay, North Carolina
> 919-555-4515

Search Consultant:

Enclosed is a résumé of my background and experience in general management.

In ten years as C.E.O. of the Connerfield Corporation, whose net sales were $350 million, my achievements have been striking and significant. My income is in the low six figures.

I am now seeking new and challenging responsibilities in an organization with similar needs.

Should you have a client assignment matching my background or would like to set up a mutually convenient appointment, please contact me at the above address.

> Sincerely,

/cu
Enclosure   Richard L. Jones

SEARCH

Anne C. Whitby
32-28 Sixth Avenue
Minneapolis, Minn 00416

Mr. Walter Mays
Execusearch, Inc.
3rd Street
Chicago, Illinois 10042

Dear Mr. Mays:

Enclosed is a copy of my résumé for review against your client assignments.

As shown by my résumé, I have an excellent track record as Marketing Director in businesses with sales volumes of up to $100 million, and in industries ranging from book publishing to electronics and optical products distribution. About half of my last twelve years have been spent as an effective line and staff manager in international businesses.

My current compensation is $52,000.

During the business day, I can be reached at (800) 888-1707.

Very truly yours,

/cu
Enclosure   Anne C. Whitby

Most search firms, regardless of their size, assign a given search to a single consultant. At the larger companies, unsolicited résumés are screened by researchers. They know enough about their firm's current business to give the individual handling a particular search assignment the résumés of people who seem to meet its requirements. The consultant looks through these résumés and decides whether he will contact the individuals they describe. At smaller firms, the consultant may be his own researcher, in which case one step is removed from the process.

Unsolicited résumés are becoming an increasingly important resource for the executive search business. If a résumé comes in which doesn't match a current search but looks as if it might meet future needs, the firm may keep the document on file for about six months. After that period, it is considered to be out-of-date and is normally discarded. When a firm accepts a new assignment, the consultant's first move will be to check the files for appropriate résumés. He'll also contact people who have been reliable sources for good prospects in the past.

In a normal search, a consultant will turn up about fifty people who meet the job requirements to one degree or another. As he compares résumés, he may narrow the field to half that number and call the remaining individuals to screen them in telephone interviews.

If you receive such a call, you'll be asked specific questions about your résumé, track record, skills, and goals. If you didn't offer salary information when you contacted the search firm, you may be asked for it at this time. You may also be asked to give a more detailed description of your work experience than your résumé provides.

If you survive the telephone screening—and eight to ten people probably will—you'll be asked to come to the search firm for an interview. Once again, the search executive will try to determine how well your abilities fit the requirements of the job he has been assigned to fill. He'll also want to find out whether you are articulate, and he'll want to be assured that you look presentable and act appropriately in an interview situation.

Personal chemistry begins to enter the selection process at this point. The consultant probably isn't enough of a specialist to know all the specific requirements of the job in question, so he won't make his decision only on the basis of skills and experience. Nor will he be able to determine just how the decision-makers at the client company will react to you personally, so he can't reach a decision on chemistry alone. It's likely that he'll draw a general conclusion about you and that will color his recommendation. If you don't impress him, he won't send you on to see his client.

After this round of interviews, the search executive will narrow his list of candidates to three or four choices and inform his client of his selections. He may rank the finalists and pass this information along as well.

If you reach this stage of the process, you will probably be invited to the company for an interview. If you are asked to return for a second interview, you're likely to be either the first or second choice for the job.

As you can see, the search process proceeds along very specific lines. It uses a rifle-shot approach to match people to jobs. Search consultants have well-defined slots to fill, and they rarely deviate from these strict job specifications. In addition, the process is as much an art as it is a science. You can be removed from the search at a number of points along the way for a variety of subjective as well as objective reasons.

As a result, when you deal with search firms, you have to anticipate a high rejection rate, which you shouldn't take personally. Expect to receive form letters that begin, "We have nothing at this time," or, in many instances, expect to hear nothing at all. Search firms receive stacks of unsolicited résumés each week, and many organizations cut their paperwork substantially by contacting only those people whose résumés match the requirements of an existing search. There is nothing personal behind the treatment—or lack of treatment—you receive. It's simply the way the system works.

If you land an interview with a search firm, exploit it. Don't think only in terms of a single job opportunity. Sell yourself to the search firm. If you don't get past a telephone screening, write a note to the search consultant, thank him for his interest and tell him you hope you'll be able to work together in the future. Consultants do retain an interest in candidates who impress them, and they do like to increase their business. The combination sometimes prompts search executives to call one or more of their corporate clients and say, "I realize that you don't have any searches on right now, but I've just talked with a person I think you really ought to meet."

Employment Agencies

Since search firms typically limit their activities to jobs at or above the $50,000 level, and since employment agencies have traditionally handled jobs ranging up to about $30,000 or $40,000, there is an apparent no-man's land for job-seekers between the two levels. If you are looking for work in the $35,000 to $50,000 range, you would be wise to contact both the leading employment agencies and the small- to medium-sized search firms.

But even if you want a job that comes with a $60,000 price tag, you shouldn't neglect employment agencies entirely. Some companies choose not to pay the hefty fees that search firms command, sending their business to employment agencies instead. These agencies earn their fees only when an individual they recommend is actually hired by a company. The client pays nothing up front and, as a result, can list an opening with as many agencies as it wishes. Finally, the fees charged by employment agencies are usually substantially less than those charged by search firms.

Employment agencies must, as a result, operate quite differently than search firms. Since they receive smaller percentages of smaller starting salaries, since they aren't paid until someone is hired, and since they often compete with other agencies to fill the same jobs, they typically have to hustle to be successful.

If you visit an employment agency, don't expect much in the way of kid-glove treatment. You'll probably be given a quick interview, where you'll discuss your résumé and your objectives with an agency representative. A few agencies are populated by harried, unpleasant individuals who frown and ask questions like, "What do you have to offer me?" or, "Who are you, anyway?" If an agency has a listing that is somewhat below your qualifications and outside your interests, a commission-starved representative may try to bully you into considering it by saying, "Golly, I just don't see how you're qualified for the kinds of jobs you want." In a situation like this, remember that you've gone through a detailed planning process to determine your goals. He or she hasn't.

For every employment agency ogre, there are many more representatives who are genuinely interested in pointing you toward job opportunities that meet your needs. But don't expect anyone at an agency to be able to devote too much time to your cause. And certainly don't put up with anyone who tries to fast-talk you into an unsuitable job.

There are other reasons for being selective as you choose employment agencies. Make sure you have a clear understanding with a firm that it won't arbitrarily send your résumé to companies. If you were to list yourself with ten agencies, and if each shotgunned your résumé indiscriminately, a single employer could receive your résumé ten times. This doesn't make you appear to be very exclusive, although it does show that you are serious about finding a job. More important, it may raise a real problem for a would-be employer. If he decides to hire you, which of the ten agencies gets the fee? Will all ten argue that they saw you first? An employer may solve this problem by not hiring you—or not even interviewing you.

Be selective with your employment agency choices. Tell those you decide to work with that you only want to be considered for existing openings.

"Career Services" Agencies

The business pages of many newspapers contain ads for companies that are neither search firms nor employment agencies. The ads describe hazily defined services ranging from "executive marketing" and "job marketing" to "career services" or "career management." The individuals who offer these programs may call themselves "search consultants," although they shouldn't be confused with representatives of executive search firms. We've even seen one ad in which the organization awards its counselors the title "job search activator," whatever that may be.

People in our business have a more prosaic name for these companies. We call them "retail outfits," and we stress the word "retail." They sell job-search services direct to individuals.* A real problem with some of them is that they spend much more time and energy marketing these services than delivering them. They may play on the vulnerabilities of people who have just lost jobs and will grasp at almost any straw to replace them.

As a result, the retail job counseling business has earned a generally poor reputation for itself. Some of these firms tend to charge a great deal of money for simple résumé services. We talked to one man who left a job paying $21,000 a year, contacted a retail firm, and was told that its services would cost him $5,000—25% of his annual salary.

Some of the companies are very successful, however, and have grown dramatically in recent years. It seems unlikely that they could record such progress without satisfying at least some of their clients some of the time.

But when we hear people recount the particularly unpleasant experiences they've had at the hands of these out-

---

* At companies like Drake Beam Morin, individual clients must be sponsored by corporations or other organizations, and the sponsor must pay the cost of the client's program.

fits, we begin to wonder. Perhaps some persons want jobs so badly that they expect too much from the firms. But, too often, it seems that people are promised the sun and the moon, spend thousands of dollars to get them, and, for their money, receive hastily written résumés and lists of "contacts" that have been copied from the pages of readily available business directories.

Our advice is to stay away from these retail firms. We feel that it is unlikely that they can offer anything that you can't achieve for yourself. But we also understand that, if you feel that you're getting nowhere by yourself as you search for a job, you may be tempted to look to them for help. If you do, proceed cautiously. Make sure you understand what you will get and how much it will cost.

If a representative of a retail firm suggests that he can find a job *for* you, run out the door. If he hints that he knows a quick and easy process that will find you a job, head for cover. If he tells you that he'll write your résumé for you, distribute it, and put you in touch with companies that are sitting and waiting for you to come to work for them, don't believe a word he says, no matter how comforting such a miracle may sound.

If, on the other hand, he lets you know that while his company can help, you are the only person who can find you a job, then he's being honest. If he stresses the development of a personal contact network as a central ingredient to your job search—and tells you that you'll have to create it yourself—then he is being realistic. If he guarantees (in writing) that you'll receive substantial interview training, at least three to five hours of one-on-one practice that includes a trained counselor and video-tape replays, then he may be offering you something for your money. But is it worth the cost, since you'll have to do most of the work?

To evaluate a retail firm, ask to meet the man or woman who will actually be your counselor. Initially, you will most likely be introduced to a marketing representative who may be more interested in closing a sale than giving you realistic advice. You need to speak to the individual who will work with you day-in and day-out. See if you feel comfortable with that person. Make sure that he or she will work with you throughout the program.

Be skeptical of firms that stress a great deal of psychological testing. Make sure that it is conducted by trained, competent counselors. In the wrong hands, psychological tests can do damage. Some firms use them only because they keep their clients busy.

Finally, be sure to discover exactly what you will receive for your money. Some retail firms work through a staged process. You pay a certain amount for an initial "career assessment." When that's completed, you learn that if you *really* want to find a job, you should let the agency's "marketing committee" sit around a table and ask you questions. That costs more, of course. This "Chinese menu" approach can turn out to be very expensive.

It is unfortunate but true that an individual is most likely to be attracted by a retail firm's promises when he is least able to be discriminating about the value of the services that are offered. If you are about to sign up with one of these agencies, consider a few options before you act. Could a psychologist trained in vocational counseling give you more service for less money? Would it be sensible to simply wait a week before signing a contract, just to make sure that you aren't putting yourself in a questionable position and looking for a magical way to a new job?

Personal Contact Networks: The 70% Solution

One job search tactic—which involves no magic—accounts for 70% of all the jobs that our clients accept. It's called networking, and with it, a job-seeker constructs a search network by talking to friends and business associates who introduce him to a continually expanding circle of personal contacts. We've watched thousands of individuals find good new jobs by building networks that expand through the business universe until the person meets the job he or she has been looking for. It sounds mysterious and isn't.

You begin the process by making a list of thirty or fifty or even one hundred people with whom you are acquainted. Your first thought is likely to be, "I can't possibly come up with that many names." You probably can. The people do not have to come from the field or fields you have targeted. You simply want to find out whether they know anyone in or near those fields. If you are looking for a job in the data-processing business, for instance, your lawyer and your accountant would be excellent people to list, since they may have friends, clients, or advisers who work in the field.

Your list can include doctors, ministers, next-door neighbors, old friends, girlfriends, old girlfriends, boyfriends, casual acquaintances, former classmates, former teachers, former clients, placement officers, bankers, stockbrokers, people who work at professional associations, consultants you've met at search firms, fellow club members, even your dentist. (Imagine the captive audience he commands in a day.) Don't limit yourself or be too restrictive. If a name comes into your head, write it down. You can always erase it later in the game if it really makes no sense.

When you've exhausted your address book and your memory (and your spouse's memory as well), divide the names into primary and secondary categories. If you decide that there is a better than average chance that an individual will know someone in the field you have targeted, put his name in the primary pile. If a person seems somewhat less likely to be able to assist you, his name goes on the secondary list. Don't get carried away with this process, however, since it's only a loose way to set priorities and organize the first level of your network.

Starting with your list of primary names, you will contact each person you've identified and try to set up a short personal meeting. If the individual is a close friend or business acquaintance, you can probably pick up the phone and call for an appointment. As you expand your network and it begins to include the names of people you've never met, you may want to initiate contacts by sending out letters and following up with phone calls to arrange meetings.

This is the point at which most of our clients balk. "Oh no," they say, "I couldn't ask any of those people for a job."

They certainly couldn't, and they certainly shouldn't.

In fact, before they make their first calls or send out their first letters, we make them memorize the first rule of the networking process: Never ask for a job, always ask for suggestions. Don't ask for favors, ask for advice.

Even your best friends don't want you to ask them for a job. They really don't even want to hear that you're out of work. They don't want you to tell them how upset you are, and they don't want you to add your problems to the problems they already have. If you ask anyone for a job, you're putting someone on the spot. He or she will find remarkably creative reasons for not being able to see you.

Suppose, however, that you call and say, "I'm in the process of making a career change, and I'd like to take fifteen minutes of your time to ask some questions and get some advice." You've removed the risk from the situation for that person, because he or she knows that all you want is advice. *Everyone* loves to give advice. People write books just to be able to give advice. You make people happy by asking for advice, because you award them a coveted title: *Consultant*.

When you call people, you shouldn't even let them imagine that you might ask for a job. Be blunt. Say, "I want to reassure you that I'm not going to ask you to find me a job. I'd like information from you, and I'd like to learn whether you can recommend other people I should talk with."

That is the key to the networking process. Each time you meet a new contact, your hope is that he or she will be able to recommend you to someone else. This keeps your network growing, and, at some point in the process, it will cause a job opportunity to surface.

Try for face-to-face meetings. Ask to meet the person in his office. Avoid lunch meetings or getting together for a drink after work. In an office, you can take notes, your contact can make notes, and he will have at hand the tools that you hope will be used—an address book and a telephone.

Keep the meeting brief and to the point. Try to take up no more than fifteen minutes of your contact's time. Spend that period concentrating on the subject at hand—your career.

Be prepared to deliver a three-minute summary of what you've done and what you intend to do next in your career. As you discuss your experience, mention a few of your major strengths and accomplishments. As you talk about the future, be as clear as you can about the direction you want it to take.

If the contact is employed in your target industry, find out as much as you can about what is happening in that business. Is it expanding or shrinking? What companies are doing well? What might someone with your qualifications and objectives expect to receive in salary?

If the individual is not employed in the field you have targeted, ask whether he knows people who are. If he does not, persist. Ask whether he can think of people he has dealt with who could introduce you to other people who actually do work in your target industry. If you prepare a series of polite, open-ended questions of this type, your contact will probably find that he does, in fact, know one or two people who can help you move closer to your target.

What you want him to say is, "Yes, I can think of three people you should talk to." What you want him to do is to give these individuals a call on your behalf. If he does, you've started to expand your network. If he doesn't, ask whether you can use his name to give them a call on your own. This calls for a bit of courage, but remember that people do like to help other people and are flattered when others seek their counsel.

Your goal is to come away from each appointment with two things. First, you want your contact to remember you and your skills so that, if he hears about something in the future, or if he discovers a need for someone with your abilities in his own organization, he'll think of you. Second, you hope that he will pass you along to two or three other people, so that you can continue the process. You'll take one new name, of course, or even none: Something may still come from this contact in the future.

Suppose that you contact twenty-five people to start, and each of them introduces you to two more people. All of a sudden, your network has seventy-five members and is expanding geometrically. Your skills, interests, and, most important, your availability become known to a larger and larger group of people. And since you're not just passed along to anyone, but to individuals who work in or close to your targeted field, your network actually gets more precisely defined as it gets bigger. The quality and quantity of your contacts improve.

You have to be a good bookkeeper to make the process function properly. If you let your network get away from you, it will self-destruct. Follow-up is all-important. You need to know which individuals to contact next and which are owed thank-you letters for having taken the time to help you. Keep a series of file cards or use a notebook to retain a tight grip on the process. Jotting down the following information will help you stay on top of things:

NAME: INTRODUCED BY:

PHONE:

TITLE/COMPANY:

ADDRESS:

INITIAL CONTACT: (date and how followed up)

ADDITIONAL CONTACT: (date and nature of contact)

It is also important to prepare yourself in advance for every stage in the networking process. Suppose you're ready to telephone someone at the suggestion of one of your pri-

mary contacts. Try to plan the conversation by anticipating
the direction it might take and preparing questions and answers to help keep it on track. For example, once you've
identified yourself, you might expect your new contact to ask
an obvious question: "What can I do for you?"

Use the question to build a bridge. You might say, "I'm
calling at the suggestion of John Jones, an associate of mine
who speaks very highly of your expertise in the data-processing field." Now you and your contact have something in common—John Jones.

Your contact might reply, "That's very nice of John to
say. Why did he refer you to me?"

This is the time to ask for advice. Be ready with a statement like, "I'm looking for an objective viewpoint from
someone with your background about the future of the data-
processing business. I'd like advice about opportunities that
may exist there, since I'm in the process of making a career
change. Let me make it clear that I'm not calling to ask for a
job, however, I'm simply looking for information."

Your new contact is likely to say, "I'd be happy to do
what I can." If he does, you have gained your first objective—
his involvement.

You might respond, "Before I start my job search in
earnest, I'd appreciate some thoughts and comments about
my résumé. I want to make sure that my objectives come
across clearly, and I'd like to be certain that the personal
accomplishments I mention are in line with the needs of the
industry. Can we schedule a fifteen-minute meeting to talk in
your office?"

If the man agrees to the meeting, you've added another
layer to your network. If he doesn't, he may ask, "Do you
have any questions I can answer over the phone?" Be ready
with several, and give some thought to the order in which
you ask them, regardless of whether you raise them in person
or on the phone.

Start with "yes" questions, inquiries that your contact

ought to be able to answer. You might ask, "What's the direction of data processing in the '80s?" or, "Are any companies having difficulty keeping up with the industry?" or, "Do you know of any companies that are growing rapidly and may be expanding their operations?" You can expect that the individual will be able to come up with answers to all these questions.

Then you can move on to "possibly no" questions, queries that the man might not know an answer for. You might say, "In the course of my research, I've selected five companies that appear to have excellent data-processing operations. I don't know a great deal about any of them, however, and I wonder if you can tell me anything about their operations and managements."

The sequence is important. If you begin by asking a string of questions that your contact doesn't have answers for, you run two risks. He may wonder, "Why is this person asking me about things I know nothing about? Is he dumb?" Or you might put him on the defensive: "Why don't I know the answers to these questions? Am I dumb? I think I should get out of this meeting." Either way, you lose.

If the contact doesn't raise the issue, your final question should be, "Will you help me with introductions to some of the people we've discussed?" If no names have come up, ask whether the man can supply any. You are trying, of course, to continue the expansion of your network.

If you choose to introduce yourself to a new contact by writing a letter, make it specific. First, tell how you got to this person by naming the individual who brought up the contact's name. Then go straight to the point. Describe your background in a short paragraph. Define your career goals in another. Say that you would appreciate getting some information about companies and individuals in the field you have targeted. Ask if the person will take fifteen minutes to talk to you. Say that you'll call for an appointment.

Don't make a pest of yourself by writing a six-page story

of your life. Don't ramble. Don't expect to get favorable responses to your letters if you imply that you're looking for someone to do a lot of work for you.

And, as you move from contact to contact, be sure that you don't embarrass anyone. Get clearance before you use a person's name to get in touch with someone else. If someone isn't willing to help, don't say, "Well, Harry said that you'd be happy to see me." Be sensitive to the fact that you are now representing other people.

The Evolution of a Job

As you think about the concept of personal contact networks, you may ask, "Why am I spreading myself out among all these people? I need a job, not an extended family."

To understand how and why the process works, you need to understand something about how jobs evolve. Imagine that you are at the other end of the process: You have an opening to fill.

That's a problem. You, or someone else in your organization, must cover that slot and perform those duties until the position is filled. You probably have move than enough to occupy your days as it is. To put anyone in that position, you'll have to assume a certain amount of risk, because you'll have to live with the consequences.

You're contending with two conflicting forces. First, with time: The longer it takes to hire someone, the more additional work you and your staff must do. So you want to fill the slot quickly. But there is also a "need-to-know" dimension to the situation. You're looking for skills—the things an individual can do, and how well he or she can do them. And you have to make decisions about chemistry—how well an individual will fit into your organization.

The first thing that most people do in this situation is to call friends and associates. You announce how desperately you need to find someone to fill this job, and you ask your friends whether they know *anyone* who might fit the bill. If someone you respect says, "I know *just* the person . . ." you've cut your risk and lessened your anxiety considerably, and in a very short time. You have an expert opinion about a candidate. That puts you well up the "need-to-know" scale.

Consider the alternatives. Your firm's personnel department will probably give you a stack of résumés which will probably tell you what someone wants you to hear, not what you need to know.

If you take out a want-ad, you're likely to be swamped with applicants who may or may not meet your needs. There's no real way to find out without conducting endless interviews, and the time that could take makes you wince.

Going to a search firm will improve your odds to a certain degree, but that is an expensive proposition. And, anyway, how can you be certain that a search consultant will really understand your needs?

Your best option seems to be getting in touch with everyone you know.

The Advantage of Networking

Now return to your own situation and consider your position as a job-seeker. The more contacts you've made as you built your network, the more likely it is that your name will come up in an "I-know-just-the-person" conversation. And, as you are introduced to more and more people in your target industry, the chances improve that you'll walk into the office of someone who *already* needs your services.

The value of the networking process is that you are constantly advertising yourself. It's comparable to putting up point-of-purchase displays at the end of the aisle in a supermarket. You're not just sitting on the third shelf from the left in aisle six, waiting to be recognized. You're creating your own recognition points.

You talk to John, and he sends you off to see Henry. When John and Henry meet for lunch two weeks later, John may ask whether Henry saw you. Henry may say, "Yes, but you know, now that I think of it, I should have put him in touch with Jim." So Henry calls you back, your network continues to grow and, all of a sudden, someone you've contacted hears about a job and thinks about you. You land an interview, and that is the goal of your marketing strategy.

The Hidden Job Market

Another benefit of the networking process is that it admits you to that almost mythical place—the hidden job market. The term refers to a sizable part of the employment universe in which jobs have not yet crystallized into official openings but where their need is beginning to be felt within an organization.

These opportunities are likely to surface:

- In organizations that are performing poorly and could stand new leadership.
- In departments that have fallen behind in their assigned responsibilities because of a lack of adequate staff or a shortage of competent leadership.
- In organizations where growth, expansion, new products or new services have created needs for new positions.

Until these needs are defined—and the opening moves into the visible job market—they obviously won't be advertised in newspapers or listed with search firms. A company mailing could trigger someone's thought processes, but it is much more likely that, as an individual expands his network, the growing knowledge of his skills and his availability will become known to someone who wonders, "Could he help *us* out? We really could use someone with those skills."

Many people are misled by discussions of the hidden job market. It does not refer to hundreds or thousands of existing jobs which, for some dark reason, have been kept secret. It does not represent empty chairs or vacant offices that are waiting for bodies to fill them. This sort of misconception causes people to think and, sadly enough, even to say, "You must have a job somewhere in this place for me. I've read all about the hidden job market."

But it does exist, occurring when organizations accumulate new needs that have not been planned for. You can capitalize on this phenomenon because, as you meet more and more people through the networking process, you give them the opportunity to match your skills to their needs. You're not trying to fit yourself into someone else's predetermined slot. You're describing what it is that *you* are looking for. This gives you flexibility that other job-hunting techniques simply don't offer.

Finally, it lets others find out who you are and what you can do in an environment that is much more comfortable and less stress-filled than the traditional, high-anxiety "Job Interview."

7 * The Interview

THE selection interview is certainly the most important event in the job search and, for many people, the most intimidating step in the entire employment process. The activities that lead to this event—from creating résumés to building contact networks—aim for the same general goal: landing interviews with targeted companies or organizations. Now the focus shifts, and a new objective emerges: using the interview to get the job itself.

The interview marks the climax of the job campaign.* Obviously, no matter how well you plan your search or prepare yourself during the weeks and months that precede the interview phase, all that time and energy really pay off only when you get a job that you've been aiming for. This is done—or not done—at the job interview, and that is why the experience can seem to be such an unnerving, "do-or-die" confrontation.

But it doesn't have to be that way. In fact, by following the systematic process that we have described in this book, you not only work toward arranging interviews, but you also

---

* It isn't the final step, however. An offer must be made, negotiated, and accepted to seal the job. But the position is won or lost in the interview.

prepare yourself so that you can turn these meetings to your advantage. If you think of an interview as an isolated incident in the campaign to find a new job, it certainly can inspire terror. But if you realize that everything you do to land an interview also prepares you to conduct it effectively, then it becomes the logical next step in the process. You become more confident that you can use it as an opportunity rather than experience it as an inquisition.

For instance, one common interview question that can turn aggressive businessmen into quivering stutterers isn't even asked as a question: "Tell me about yourself!" an interviewer demands with a menacing grin.

If you haven't thought about the question, it may stump you. What is the interviewer really looking for? What should you say about yourself? How long should you talk? How on earth can you distill your life into a single coherent answer? The possibilities for hemming and hawing seem limitless.

But even if you haven't anticipated the question, you really have given it a substantial amount of thought. Since you left your last job, you have probably come to know yourself better than at any time in the recent past. You've dealt with troublesome emotions, and you've weathered a difficult psychological storm. You've investigated your past as you listed career accomplishments and prepared a résumé. You've anticipated your future by considering your personal and professional needs as you targeted your job search.

You may even have practiced your answer. As you built your personal contact network, you undoubtedly talked about yourself with the people you met. You probably refined your comments in subsequent meetings, distilling your responses as you learned what was most persuasive and what seemed to miss the point. As you discovered what worked and what didn't, you became more confident with your answers and more comfortable in your discussions.

Now, as you get ready for formal selection interviews, you can adapt several activities from this informal process to improve your performance during job interviews. Specifically, you can:

- Anticipate questions,
- Prepare answers, and
- Practice, practice, practice.

First, you can anticipate questions that are likely to be asked. A job interview is generally a planned event in which the interviewer seeks to obtain various kinds of information about the candidate. This data doesn't change a great deal from one interview to another. As a result, the same questions are frequently asked in different interviews. You can predict them, a process that will obviously remove much of the uncertainty from the actual interview.

If you have a good idea of the questions that are likely to be asked, you can prepare answers for them so that you won't be caught flat-footed—without any response—and so that you won't ramble on incoherently as you search for an acceptable answer.

Finally, when you've prepared an answer, you can practice it so that you will respond confidently and concisely in a real interview. This practice can include not only what you say but also the manner in which you present yourself and the way in which you deliver your answers.

Anticipation

Think back to your days at school. On the night before at least one final examination, didn't you imagine how nice life would be if only you knew the questions on the next day's test? Here's your chance.

A good interview is not a haphazard event. A competent interviewer will have planned the occasion carefully, dividing the interview into sections, preparing questions to be asked in each segment and, in general, orchestrating the affair so that a variety of predetermined subjects and lines of inquiry will be covered in detail.

By analyzing the interviewer's probable plan, you can anticipate a number of the questions. To discuss this topic, we will draw from an interview model created by Henry Morgan and John Cogger for Drake Beam Morin, Inc., which describes a particularly well-planned interview.* Not all interviews show such professional preparations, but almost any hiring discussion will touch some of the subjects described below. In general, the better trained the interviewer, the more closely the interview will approximate this format.

Morgan and Cogger divide their model interview into six general sections: an introduction, a section on work experience, questions about education, a discussion of present activities and interests, a summary of strengths and shortcomings, and a section devoted to closing remarks.

The introductory section of the interview begins, understandably enough, with a greeting. A good interviewer acts like a gracious host, introducing himself and offering a cordial greeting and a firm handshake. This begins to establish the warm relationship that marks superior interviews, as the interviewer attempts to reduce anxiety and characterize the session to follow as a friendly, rather than adversarial, event. The effective interviewer's greeting is genuine, not contrived. He or she knows that an insincere atmosphere can cripple the confident exchange of information that is the basis of a good interview.

Next, the interviewer devotes a few moments to small talk. If he notices on your résumé that you are interested in sports, he might discuss a recent event. If he is acquainted with people at one of the companies where you've worked in the past, he may attempt to discover whether you share friends in common. This part of the interview is also

---

* Morgan and Cogger's *The Interviewer's Manual,* published by Drake Beam Morin, Inc., investigates the ways in which professional interviewers plan and conduct interviews in greater detail than we mention here. You can obtain a copy by sending a check for $15.95 to: Professional Educational Materials, A Division of Drake Beam Morin, Inc., 277 Park Avenue, New York, NY 10172.

designed to help reduce the tensions that are natural to the situation. During the warm-up period, the interviewer phrases his questions so that you do most of the talking. He realizes that the simple act of hearing your own voice can relax you and make you feel less self-conscious.

Once the conversation appears to be flowing smoothly, the interviewer moves on to the next section of the interview with one or two opening questions. These initial queries may explore your expectations about the job, or they may deal with the events that led to the interview. The questions can range from the ubiquitous, "Tell me about yourself!" to one or more of the following examples:

- What has been your contact with our organization?
- What do you know about this job and about this company?
- How did you come to be interested in this job?
- What is your understanding of the purpose of this interview?
- Tell me, what led up to your coming to see me today?

The interviewer uses your answers to determine whether you and he are operating from the same set of assumptions about the purpose of the interview. He either confirms or attempts to alter your expectations so that you and he establish a joint goal for the meeting.

While this part of the interview seeks to relax you and set the stage for questions to come, it also addresses several important priorities. In the opening moments, the interviewer is likely to watch you and interpret your initial responses in an attempt to draw some conclusions about your appearance and general manner, your skills of self-expression, and your responsiveness to the situation. Right from the start, he begins to form an impression.

In fact, many people argue that the most critical portion of an interview is the first five minutes. The interviewer has already seen your résumé. He may have talked to a search firm representative about you. If this isn't your initial interview with the organization, he may have discussed you with other people in the firm. So he knows a substantial amount about you before you've even walked into his office. Now, beginning with the first handshake, he's looking carefully to see how you handle yourself.

As the interviewer begins the body of the interview, he may say something like:

I'd like to talk with you about your background and experience. If I get to know you well—both what you've done and what you hope to do—we can judge whether there are opportunities in our organization that are suited to your talents and interests. It's certainly to your advantage, as well, that we become well acquainted. We both need to be able to make intelligent employment decisions.

So I'd like to hear about your jobs and schooling, your hobbies and interests, and anything else you'd like to tell or ask me. Perhaps the best place to start is with your work experience.

The most important part of this statement is that it recognizes the fact that a good interview is a shared discussion. The interviewer expects to find out certain things about you, and he understands that you expect to find out certain things about the organization.

Next, the interviewer begins his questions about your work experience. In this section of the interview—and in each subsequent area of inquiry—he is likely to begin with a prepared "lead" question. These questions announce clearly and briefly what he expects to discuss in a particular interview segment. In the section on work experience, the lead question might be:

Tell me about the jobs you've held, what your duties and responsibilities were, and what you liked or didn't like about them. I'm also interested in your level of earnings, any special achievements you may have had, and what you think you gained from these jobs.

Let's begin with your earliest jobs—those you may have had after school or during summer vacations. What do you remember about your very first job?

From these early jobs, the interviewer will proceed to details about your military service (if it is applicable), to the full-time positions you have held and to volunteer work you may have done. As he probes your career, he'll draw from an arsenal of specific questions:

- What things did you do best in that job?
- What things did you do less well?
- What things did you like best there?
- What did you like less well?
- What were your major achievements in that position?
- How did you achieve them?
- What were the most difficult problems you faced?
- How did you deal with them?
- In what ways do you think that you were most effective with people there?
- Were there ways in which you were less effective?
- What was your level of earnings?
- What did you learn from that work experience?
- What were you looking for in that job?
- What are you looking for in your career?
- What are your short- and long-term goals?

The interviewer is unlikely to ask each question about each job you've held. Some may not be raised at all. But if he is a good interviewer, he'll ask questions like these to determine how your work history can be related to the job being discussed. Is what you've done relevant to this job? Has your work experience given you sufficient experience for the job in question? Do you seem to possess the skills and competence called for by this position?

He'll also be looking at you in terms of adaptability, productivity, and apparent motivation. He'll consider your leadership qualities, and he may try to assess the degree of growth and development that has characterized your career.

The next topic in the interview is education. Here, the lead question might be:

You've given me a good picture of your work experience. Now let's discuss your education. I'd like to know a little about your early schooling and then, of course, more about your more recent education, including any specialized training you've had. I'm interested in such things as the subjects you preferred, those you didn't like as well, your grades, the extracurricular activities you became involved in and any special recognition you received. Let's begin with your earliest schooling. What was it like?

In this section, the interviewer might refer all the way back to your elementary schooling, then spend somewhat more time talking about your high school and college years, and conclude the section by investigating specialized training you may have received or recent courses you may have taken. He may ask such questions as:

- What were your best subjects?
- In which subjects did you do less well?
- What subjects did you like most?
- Which did you like least?
- How did you feel about your teachers?
- What kind of grades did you receive?
- How much effort did you put into getting them?
- What were some of your reasons for choosing that school?
- What was your major field there?
- What special achievements did you record?
- What were the toughest problems you faced?
- What kinds of extracurricular activities were you engaged in?
- How did you finance your education?
- How do you think your education relates to your career?

- How do you feel about further schooling or specialized training?

As he asks these questions and considers your answers, the interviewer thinks in terms of the relevance of your education to the job. He considers the sufficiency of your schooling and tries to take some measure of your intellectual abilities. He looks at the breadth and depth of your knowledge and the level of accomplishment you achieved during your school years. He considers versatility, motivation, and specific interests. He may try to determine how your education might affect or determine the way you react to authority, and he may also think about leadership qualities and teamwork abilities.

The next part of the model interview is devoted to present activities and interests. This is often considered an optional topic, as many organizations are not too interested in hobbies or leisure pursuits. In any event, this sort of personal information is only relevant if it can be related to the job under discussion. The lead question might be:

We've talked about your work and schooling. Now let's talk about your leisure activities—your interests and hobbies. What do you do for fun and recreation, either on your own or with others?

Here, the interviewer covers special interests and hobbies as well as civic and community affairs that might be relevant to the job. He may discuss issues related to your health and energy, and he could use this section to ask about geographical preferences you may have. His questions may include:

- What kinds of things do you like to do in your spare time?
- To what extent are you involved in your community?
- Do you have any kinds of health problems that might affect your job performance?
- What would be your reaction to relocating?

- How do you feel about business travel?
- Can you think of any circumstances that might influence your job performance?

As he asks these questions, the interviewer looks for such things as vitality, maturity, and good judgment. He is interested in determining how well you manage your time, your energy, and even your money. He is concerned about intellectual growth, cultural breadth, and the diversity of your interests. He thinks in terms of the social effectiveness of how you act and what you do outside your job. He may use the questions to assess interpersonal skills and interests, your sense of leadership, even your basic values and goals as they are reflected in your leisure activities.

Next, the interviewer moves to one of the most important sections of the selection interview—a summary of strengths and shortcomings. He is likely to divide this discussion into two parts, and he will probably begin each with a lead question. He starts with your strengths:

Now let's try to summarize our discussion. As you think about what we've covered, what would you say are some of your chief strengths? Here's your chance to brag a little! What are some of the assets that would make you a good prospect for any employer?

Specific questions may include:

- What do you bring to a job?
- What are your main assets?
- What do you think are your major talents?
- What outstanding qualities do you see in yourself or do others see in you?
- What makes you a good investment for an employer?

Then the interviewer moves to the other side of the subject, perhaps with the aid of this lead question:

You've given me some real strengths, but what about some of your qualities that aren't so strong? All of us have a few areas we wish to improve upon. In the past, you may have had constructive criticism from friends, supervisors, or other people who know you well. Thinking of the future, what areas or what personal qualities need improvement for you to be fully effective in your job or career?

The specific questions here could include:

- What are some of your shortcomings or limitations?
- What areas do you think you should improve?
- What qualities would you like to develop further?
- What kinds of constructive criticism have you received from others?
- How might you be a risk to an employer?
- What kind of further training or experience do you think you might need?

As he asks you both sets of questions, the interviewer weighs apparent strengths against apparent weaknesses and asks himself three additional questions. Can this person do the job? (Do you have the talents, skills, knowledge, and energy for the position?) *Will* this person do the job? (Do your interests and motivation mesh with the requirements of the job?) How will this person fit in? (Will your personal qualities, character, and apparent effectiveness in social settings fit the organization's style?)

The final section of the interview is devoted to closing remarks. Here, a likely lead question might be:

You've given me a good review of your background and experience. I've enjoyed talking with you, and I appreciate your sharing this information with me. It will be of considerable value as we make our decision. Before we close, is there anything else you would like to cover? What questions would you like to ask about the job, our organization, or anything else, for that matter?

The interviewer tries to create a dialogue in this last part of the interview, answering your questions, reviewing the job and the opportunities it offers, even trying to sell you on the organization if he feels that it is appropriate to do so. He also identifies further contacts that you should make within the organization and outlines the next steps that should be taken. Finally, he offers a cordial parting, and the interview ends.

This model describes a particularly thorough selection interview. Most are not likely to be so complex or so intensive. No one can promise that you'll run into skilled interviewers everywhere you go. A trained personnel manager or human resources management executive might be expected to go into this sort of detail, in taking you all the way back to your early days in school, for instance, but it is somewhat less likely that a potential boss or immediate superior will take the time—or have the interviewing expertise—to conduct this complete an interview. But if you can handle this sort of intense interview experience, you can probably succeed at any interview.

Types of Interviews

There are four general types of interviews that you may expect to encounter as you move closer to any particular job: screening, in-depth, multiple (or "beauty parade"), and final. Each seeks to develop somewhat different sets of information, and each is likely to be conducted somewhat differently than the others.

The first in the series is the screening interview. Typically, it is conducted by a member of the organization's personnel or human resources management department. This individual cannot possibly know enough of the details about every specific position in the organization to be able to match an individual's precise qualifications to the exact demands of each job. But he or she can—and will—reach conclusions about the candidate's general experience. The interviewer will attempt to decide whether that person has the right personality for the job and the organization. He or she identifies strong and weak points and, assessing them, compares and perhaps ranks the individuals who are being considered for the position.

Don't underestimate the importance of the screening interview. It is particularly unwise to assume that you can breeze through it and begin to take matters seriously when you get to the "real" boss. If you approach a screening interview in anything but a serious and well-prepared frame of mind, the chances are good that you'll never get to see that "real" boss.

There was a time when personnel departments were considered organizational backwaters staffed with unprofessional or incompetent individuals. This is certainly not the case today. Personnel decisions and human resources planning are being taken more seriously than ever before.

This new interest in human resources management has undeniably been sparked by equal employment opportunity legislation enacted in recent years. In addition, senior management now realize that, since people are likely to be an organization's most valuable asset, it makes sense to select and nurture them as professionally as possible. The result is that intelligent, well-qualified individuals have been attracted to personnel work in recent years. Their decisions carry more weight than ever before and their observations and conclusions are taken very seriously at all levels of most organizations.

If you perform well in the screening interview, you will be invited back for an in-depth interview, which is normally conducted by the functional head or line manager in your discipline. This interview is overwhelmingly task-oriented. The manager is likely to get right down to the business at hand. He needs to satisfy himself that you know what you are talking about. The interview concentrates on the specific dimensions of the job and the interviewer tries to find out how well you fit them. Because you and the interviewer are likely to share a great deal of job-related information, this interview normally moves quickly. The interviewer grasps the points you make as readily as you understand the questions that are asked. The discussion focuses both on your technical expertise (specific job-oriented talents and experience) and on interpersonal skills.

(In some situations, the order of the screening and indepth interviews may be reversed. If you are being considered for a very high-level job, for instance, you may speak first with the functional superior and later, if all goes well, be asked to talk with a representative of the personnel staff.)

Since many organizations look for consensus before hiring individuals, successful completion of the first two rounds in the interview process is likely to result in a series of interviews which are collectively referred to as a "beauty parade." In these multiple interviews, you meet a number of people from the department or area in which you would work—individuals from higher levels, perhaps, as well as some of the people who would be your peers and subordinates within the organization. In small companies, these interviews might be scheduled with people from throughout the firm.

You may be asked to take part in a series of short private interviews with each individual, or you might find yourself sharing lunch or cocktails with a small group of people. Because they are often relaxed and unstructured affairs, these interviews can be deadly. Many capable individuals have talked themselves out of good jobs by making unguarded comments: "We should just bomb them all," or, "I think that jogging is really dumb, don't you?" or, "The problem with this country is that we've let the unions run wild." Anything you say in an interview is likely to be scrutinized. Welcome an interview conducted in a relaxed atmosphere, but don't be lulled into making thoughtless remarks. Stay alert.

If you pass this set of interviews, you are probably very close to landing the job and will be asked back for a final interview. Loose ends may be wrapped up at this time, and an offer may be made to you.

In addition to these four general types of interviews, you

may encounter other formats. You could be asked to take a psychological interview, for instance, and spend some time talking with a psychologist from the organization. You can gain an interesting perspective about the job in this situation by asking the psychologist for *his* observations about the organization.

In general, of course, the more interviews you take, the better are your chances of landing the job. Not only does being asked back indicate that the company continues to be interested in you, but, as you talk to more people there, you improve your ability to make a good decision about whether the job suits your needs and skills.

The Stress Interview

There is, however, one kind of interview that you certainly do not want to be asked to complete: the stress interview. Once quite fashionable, the stress interview has understandably and thankfully gone out of vogue in recent years. But there are undoubtedly a few people abroad who continue to think that, since anxiety and stress are part of any demanding job, it sounds like a good idea to create stress in an interview to test the candidate's reaction to it. If a job involves selling a product to difficult customers, for example, why not see how well the candidate can sell himself to a hostile or belligerent interviewer?

There are a number of problems with this approach, the principal difficulty being that creating stress in an interview is usually counterproductive. The candidate becomes defensive and resistant. The information that is elicited is limited and less candid than it would be in a more congenial atmosphere.

One of the principles of the model interview described above is that it seeks to reduce anxiety between the interviewer and the candidate. As it turns out, that is the most effective way to produce the most useful information in an interview.

Stress interviews may provoke complaints of unfair selection procedures. And since the selection interview often provides a model for the future relationships between employer and employee, a stress interview can create the undesirable situation in which a new employee starts a job full of hostile feelings for the company.

Finally, since stress encountered on the job is usually different from that which can be created in an interview, a stress interview may not even be effective in determining a candidate's ability to deal with difficult situations. It is much more productive to review the person's past behavior and attitudes about working under stress to discover this information.

How do you know if you've landed in a stress interview? The interviewer might not look at you but stare out the window throughout the discussion. You might give a carefully prepared answer to a straightforward question, only to have the interviewer respond, "No, no, you missed the point of that question entirely." An interviewer might ask embarrassing personal questions.

In a discussion of strengths and weaknesses, it is perfectly proper for an interviewer to ask about shortcomings. But if he begins the interview with the question, "What gives you the idea that you're good enough for this job?" then you are most likely in for a difficult experience.

To deal with a stress interview, meet the situation head-on. Let the interviewer know that you know what is taking place. Do not, under any circumstances, sit and try to answer demeaning questions. Don't put up with impolite behavior. If the interviewer won't look at you, you might say, "It seems that we have a problem here. I'd be much more comfortable if you'd look at me as we talk."

If an interviewer is obviously trying to goad you by contesting your answers or actively trying to make you uncomfortable, get up and leave the interview. As you head for the door, you might say something like, "If the purpose of all this is to find out whether I can deal with aggressive situations, the answer is yes. But if you think that you have the right to act this way, the answer is no."

The interviewer will almost certainly drop the pose and continue the interview on more considerate terms. He'll have found out that you can deal with aggression, so you'll have passed the test.

But even if you do pass, remember that an organization using stress interview techniques is likely to have an extremely aggressive management style. Ask yourself whether you really want to get involved with them. If you are an aggressive person yourself, a stress interview might not bother you at all, and the organization's style might be well-suited to you. You may even feel challenged by the situation. But be honest with yourself when you ask whether you'd like to have this sort of stress be part of your normal working day.

We recall one instance in which a job candidate created his own stress situation. He was being interviewed for a job as a corporate labor negotiator. The interviewer, a member of the company's personnel department, asked the man a question about his shortcomings or weaknesses. The man answered, "I am a labor relations expert, I have a great deal of experience, I get the job done, and I won't answer that question."

When the interviewer reported back to the vice president of labor relations the next day, he gave the man a negative appraisal. But when the vice president learned the details of the encounter, he contacted the candidate for another interview and ultimately offered him the job. That kind of behavior was exactly what he was looking for. He needed someone who wasn't afraid to say no and who wouldn't feel uncomfortable taking an unpopular stand in a difficult labor negotiation.

There is obviously a substantial amount of risk involved in this kind of behavior, however. Unless you really crave stress situations—and many people honestly do—you would be well-advised to avoid creating them and to refuse to put up with them in interviews should they occur.

Preparing Answers

As we have said, most interviews are run along more positive and supportive lines. You don't have to worry too greatly about being bushwhacked, but, at the same time, you must realize that it is the interviewer's job to discover just how effective you might be in a specific job. To be objective and impartial, he will give you every opportunity to prove yourself or to hang yourself. While a relaxed atmosphere promotes good communications, it can also lull you into lowering your guard and saying something that you never intended. You should always think before you speak.

Begin this thought process by taking the questions that are likely to be asked and preparing solid answers for them. You need to be able to answer intricate questions in a convincing manner. You need to appear knowledgeable and enthusiastic about the organization and, of course, about yourself as well.

In this section, we'll present a number of questions which we have found interesting and most likely to be asked in an interview. Many questions give you a chance to plant your foot firmly in your mouth. But, by preparing answers before you get into an interview, you can substantially reduce the likelihood of making this sort of misstep.

As we pose each question, we'll mention guidelines that may help you prepare answers. We obviously can't anticipate all of the questions or supply all of the answers ourselves. The variables of your skills and experience, and the organization's needs and goals, make that impossible.

When you have worked your way through these questions, go back to the model interview and try to prepare answers for those questions as well. The more subjects you can discuss intelligently in an interview, the less likely you are to be unpleasantly surprised.

But before you prepare your answers, consider a few general guidelines. First, make your answers as brief and concise as you can. Don't ramble. Don't over-elaborate. When you've answered the question, stop talking.

Most people worry that they will not find enough to say during an interview. Usually, the exact opposite occurs: People continue to talk long after they've answered the question. This is often caused by simple nervousness. If someone feels tense, he may speak quickly and hit a number of topics. He may decide that the more he says, the more likely he is to hit something that the interviewer will appreciate. Sometimes a candidate simply assumes that his role in an interview is to talk and that if he doesn't chatter away consistently, he isn't doing his job. It is astonishing to learn how often interviewers sum up interviews that do not turn out well for the candidate with the words, "If he'd only shut up sooner."

Second, as you prepare your answers, use positive terms whenever you can. Don't talk about a "problem." Call it a "challenge" or an "opportunity" instead.

Third, do your homework on the company or organization. As you prepare answers, tailor them to the apparent needs of the organization. Try to use specific details to show how you can help the potential employer. Get an annual report and a 10-K financial statement from the company. Talk to people who work for, sell to, or are in any way involved with the organization. If you have worked with a search firm to land the interview, ask the search executive for information about, and impressions of, the company.

Not only will this activity help you prepare specific answers, it will also help you answer an important question of your own: Is this the right job at the right company? You'll want to impress the interviewer, but you also deserve to be impressed as well.

Finally, as you consider these questions, you may wish to make notes or jot down phrases to remind you of important points you wish to cover. Avoid writing out complete answers, however. It is important to appear spontaneous and enthusiastic in an interview, and that is difficult to achieve when you repeat memorized answers. If you are comfortable with main points and key phrases, you can tailor your exact answer to the specific conditions of the interview and to the personality of the interviewer.

The Difficult Questions

1. *Tell me about yourself.*

Since this is often the opening question in an interview, be extra-careful that you don't run off at the mouth. Keep your answer to a minute or two at most. Cover four topics: early years, education, work history, and recent career experience. Emphasize this last subject. Remember that this is likely to be a warm-up question. Don't waste your best points on it.

2. *What do you know about our organization?*

You should be able to discuss products or services, revenues, reputation, image, goals, problems, management style, people, history, and philosophy. But don't act as if you know *everything* about the place. Let your answer show that you have taken the time to do some research, but don't overwhelm the interviewer, and make it clear that you wish to learn more.

You might start your answer in this manner: "In my job search, I've investigated a number of companies. Yours is one of the few that interests me, for these reasons. . . ."

Give your answer a positive tone. Don't say, "Well, everyone tells me that you're in all sorts of trouble, and that's why I'm here"—even if that *is* why you're there.

3. *Why do you want to work for us?*

The deadliest answer you can give is, "Because I like people." What else would you like—animals?

Here, and throughout the interview, a good answer comes from having done your homework so that you can speak in terms of the company's needs. You might say that your research has shown that the company is doing things you would like to be involved with, and that it's doing them in ways that greatly interest you. For example, if the organization is known for strong management, your answer should mention that fact and show that you would like to be a part of that team. If the company places a great deal of emphasis on research and development, emphasize the fact that you want to create new things and that you know this is a place in which such activity is encouraged. If the organization stresses financial controls, your answer should mention a reverence for numbers.

If you feel that you have to concoct an answer to this question—if, for example, the company stresses research, and you feel that you should mention it even though it really doesn't interest you—then you probably should not be taking that interview, because you probably shouldn't be considering a job with that organization. Your homework should include learning enough about the company to avoid approaching places where you wouldn't be able—or wouldn't want—to function. Since most of us are poor liars, it's difficult to con anyone in an interview. But even if you should succeed at it, your prize is a job you don't really want.

4.   *What can you do for us that someone else can't?*

Here you have every right, and perhaps an obligation, to toot your own horn and be a bit egotistical. Talk about your record of getting things done, and mention specifics from your résumé or list of career accomplishments. Say that your skills and interests, combined with this history of getting results, make you valuable. Mention your ability to set priorities, identify problems, and use your experience and energy to solve them.

5.   *What do you find most attractive about*
      this position? What seems least attractive about it?

List three or four attractive factors of the job, and mention a single, minor, unattractive item.

6. *Why should we hire you?*

Create your answer by thinking in terms of your ability, your experience, and your energy. (See question 4.)

7. *What do you look for in a job?*

Keep your answer oriented to opportunities at this organization. Talk about your desire to perform and be recognized for your contributions. Make your answer oriented toward opportunity rather than personal security.

8. *Please give me your definition of_____*
   [the position for which you are being interviewed].

Keep your answer brief and task-oriented. Think in terms of responsibilities and accountability. Make sure that you really do understand what the position involves before you attempt an answer. If you are not certain, ask the interviewer; he or she may answer the question for you.

9. *How long would it take you to make a meaningful contribution to our firm?*

Be realistic. Say that, while you would expect to meet pressing demands and pull your own weight from the first day, it might take six months to a year before you could expect to know the organization and its needs well enough to make a major contribution.

10. *How long would you stay with us?*

Say that you are interested in a career with the organization, but admit that you would have to continue to feel challenged to remain with any organization. Think in terms of, "As long as we both feel achievement-oriented."

11. *Your résumé suggests that you may be over-qualified or too experienced for this position. What's your opinion?*

Emphasize your interest in establishing a long-term association with the organization, and say that you assume that if you perform well in this job, new opportunities will open up for you. Mention that a strong company needs a strong staff. Observe that experienced executives are always at a premium. Suggest that since you are so well-qualified, the employer will get a fast return on his investment. Say that a growing, energetic company can never have too much talent.

12. *What is your management style?*

You should know enough about the company's style to know that your management style will complement it. Possible styles include: task-oriented ("I enjoy problem-solving: identifying what's wrong, choosing a solution and implementing it"), results-oriented ("Every management decision I make is determined by how it will affect the bottom line"), or even paternalistic ("I'm committed to taking care of my subordinates and pointing them in the right direction"). A participative style is currently quite popular: an open-door method of managing in which you get things done by motivating people and delegating responsibility.

As you consider this question, think about whether your style will let you work happily and effectively within the organization.

13. *Are you a good manager? Can you give me some examples? Do you feel that you have top managerial potential?*

Keep your answer achievement- and task-oriented. Rely on examples from your career to buttress your argument. Stress your experience and your energy.

14. *What do you look for when you hire people?*

Think in terms of skills, initiative, and the adaptability to be able to work comfortably and effectively with others. Mention that you like to hire people who appear capable of moving up in the organization.

15. *Have you ever had to fire people? What were the reasons, and how did you handle the situation?*

Admit that the situation was not easy, but say that it worked out well, both for the company and, you think, for the individual. Show that, like anyone else, you don't enjoy unpleasant tasks but that you can resolve them efficiently and—in the case of firing someone—humanely.

16. *What do you think is the most difficult thing about being a manager or executive?*

Mention planning, execution, and cost-control. The most difficult task is to motivate and manage employees to get something planned and completed on time and within the budget.

17. *What important trends do you see in our industry?*

Be prepared with two or three trends that illustrate how well you understand your industry. You might consider technological challenges or opportunities, economic conditions, or even regulatory demands as you collect your thoughts about the direction in which your business is heading.

18. *What are the "frontier issues" in our industry?*

Be prepared with two or three key issues.

19. *Why are you leaving (did you leave) your present (last) job?*

Be brief, to the point, and as honest as you can without hurting yourself. Refer back to the planning phase of your job search, where you considered this topic as you set your reference statements. If you were laid off in an across-the-board cutback, say so; otherwise, indicate that the move was your decision, the result of your action. Do not mention personality conflicts.

The interviewer may spend some time probing you on this issue, particularly if it is clear that you were terminated. The "We agreed to disagree" approach may be useful. Remember that your references are likely to be checked, so don't concoct a story for an interview.

20. *How do you feel about leaving all your benefits to find a new job?*

Mention that you are concerned, naturally, but not panicked. You are willing to accept some risk to find the right job for yourself. Don't suggest that security might interest you more than getting the job done successfully.

21. *How would you define an ideal working environment?*

Consider these values: a place where people are treated as fairly as possible, where they are given a chance to show what they can do, and where they are rewarded for their performance.

22. *How would you evaluate your present (last) firm?*

Unless it is common knowledge that the company suffers from woeful management, or that its officers are being investigated for fraud, be positive. Talk about an excellent company which gave you many fine experiences (one of which was to prepare you for a job like this one).

23. *Have you helped increase sales? Profits? How?*

Be ready with specific details from your résumé or list of career accomplishments.

24. *Have you helped reduce costs? How?*

Be prepared with quantifiable details.

25. *How much money did you account for?*

Be specific.

26. *How many people did you supervise?*

Be specific.

27. *Do you like working with figures more than with words?*

Be honest, but mention that you are comfortable with both.

28. *What do your subordinates think of you?*

Be as positive and honest as you can. Your answer can be checked easily.

29. *In your current (last) position, what features do (did) you like the most? The least?*

Be careful and be positive. Describe more features that you liked than disliked. Don't cite personality problems. If you make your last job sound terrible, an interviewer may wonder why you remained there until now.

30. *In your current (last) position, what have been (were) your five most significant accomplishments?*

Have specific examples ready. If you are asked for five examples, don't give ten accomplishments. If you want to show that you were responsible for more than five major achievements, you can say, "I've given you the five that seem most important to me. There are others if you'd like to hear them." Then, if the interviewer asks for additional accomplishments, you can give them without seeming to boast.

31. *Why haven't you found a new job before now?*

Say that finding a job is not difficult, but that finding the right job deserves time and takes careful planning.

32. *Did you think of leaving your present position before? If yes, what do you think held you there?*

You might say that the challenge of the job held you in the past, but as that seemed to disappear, you reached the decision that you should investigate other opportunities.

33. *What do you think of your boss?*

Be as positive as you can. A potential boss is likely to wonder if you might talk about him in similar terms at some point in the future.

34. *Would you describe a few situations in which your work was criticized?*

Be specific. Don't be emotional. Think in terms of constructive criticism. Show that you responded positively and benefited from the criticism.

35. *If I spoke with your boss, what would he say are your greatest strengths and weaknesses?*

Name three or four strengths and only one weakness. Be honest but not too negative. Your answer can be checked.

36. *Can you work under pressure and deal with deadlines?*

Observe that both are facts of business life. Take examples from your list of accomplishments to show how you can deal successfully with pressure and deadlines.

37. *Did you change the nature of your job?*

Tell how you improved it.

38. *Do you prefer staff (support function) or line (directly involved in the business) work? Why?*

Say that it depends on the job and its challenges.

39. *In your present (last) position, what problems did you identify that had previously been overlooked?*

Be brief and don't brag.

40. *Don't you think that you might be better-suited to a different sized company? To a different type of company?*

Tailor your answer to the job being discussed. Say that your preferences for size or type of company generally depend on the job in question. Note that your research has shown you that this organization and this job meet your criteria.

41. *If you could choose any job at any company, where would you go?*

Talk about the job and company for which you are being interviewed.

42. *Why aren't you earning more at your age?*

Say that this is one reason that you are conducting this job search. Don't be defensive.

43. *What do you feel this position should pay?*

Salary is a delicate topic. We suggest that you defer tying yourself to a precise figure for as long as you can do so politely. You might say, "I understand that the range for this job is between $_____ and $_____. That seems appropriate for the job as I understand it." You might answer the question with a question: "Perhaps you can help me on this one. Can you tell me if there is a range for similar jobs in the organization?"

If you are asked the question during an initial screening interview, you might say that you feel you need to know more about the position's responsibilities before you could give a meaningful answer to that question. Here, too, either by asking the interviewer or search executive (if one is involved), or in research done as part of your homework, you can try to find out whether there is a salary grade attached to the job. If there is, and if you can live with it, say that the range seems right to you.

If the interviewer continues to probe, you might say, "You know that I'm making $_____ now. Like everyone else, I'd like to improve on that figure, but my major interest is with the job itself." Remember that the act of taking a new job does not, in and of itself, make you worth more money.

If a search firm is involved, your contact there may be able to help with the salary question. He or she may even be able to run interference for you. If, for instance, he tells you what the position pays, and you tell him that you are earning that amount now and would like to do a bit better, he might go back to the employer and propose that you be offered an additional 10%.

If no price range is attached to the job, and the interviewer continues to press the subject, then you will have to respond with a number. You cannot leave the impression that it does not really matter, that you'll accept whatever is offered. If you've been making $80,000 a year, you can't say that a $35,000 figure would be fine without sounding as if you've given up on yourself. (If you are making a radical career change, however, this kind of disparity may be more reasonable and understandable.)

Don't sell yourself short, but continue to stress the fact that the job itself is the most important thing in your mind. The interviewer may be trying to determine just how much you want the job. Don't leave the impression that money is the only thing that is important to you. Link questions of salary to the work itself.

But whenever possible, say as little as you can about salary until you reach the "final" stage of the interview process. At that point, you know that the company is genuinely interested in you and that it is likely to be flexible in salary negotiations. For more information on this subject, refer to chapter 9.

44. *Do you have any objections to psychological tests?*

No, you would feel comfortable taking them.

45. *What other jobs or companies are you considering?*

Keep your answer related to fields that are similar to the one in which this company operates.

46. *Do you speak to people before they speak to you?*

Say that your actions depend on specific circumstances. While you wouldn't normally start a conversation with a stranger in the street, for example, you feel comfortable initiating discussions with people you don't know in normal social or business settings. The interviewer is probably trying to determine your ability to deal with unstable or unanticipated situations.

47. *What was the last book you read? Movie you saw? Sporting event you attended?*

Try to show that you lead a balanced life when answering questions like these. For example, don't say that the last book you read was a business text.

48. *Will you be out to take your boss' job?*

Say that while you certainly hope to win additional responsibility in the organization, you have always focused on getting the current job done.

49. *Are you creative?*

Be prepared with work-related examples of creativity.

50. *How would you describe your own personality?*

It may be wise to say that you are the proud possessor of a balanced personality.

51. *Do you consider yourself a leader?*

Take examples from your work experience.

52. *What are your long-range goals?*

Refer back to the planning phase of your job search. Don't answer, "I want the job you've advertised." Relate your goals to the company you are interviewing: "In a firm like yours, I would like to. . . ."

53. *What are your strong points?*

Present at least three. Use concrete, work-related examples to illustrate them. Try to relate your answer to the interviewing organization and the specific job opening.

54. *What are your weak points?*

Don't say that you have none. But try to make a negative sound like a strength carried just a bit too far: "I sometimes get impatient and become too deeply involved when we are late with a project."

Don't offer a list of weaknesses. A good interviewer is likely to press you a bit by saying, "Is there anything else?" You might say, "No, I don't think so on that topic." If he persists, come up with a second weakness, but make him ask for it. Don't offer negative information unnecessarily. If he continues on and asks for a third weakness, say politely that you really can't think of anything else.

Finally, show that you are aware of your weaknesses and are working to correct them.

55. If you could start your career again, what would you do differently?

The best answer is, "Not a thing." You should try to present yourself as an individual who is happy with his or her life. You have enjoyed its "ups" and learned from its "downs." You would not, as a result, want to change the things that brought you where you are today. Mention that it is your past, after all, which has prepared you for this position.

56. What career options do you have at the moment?

You should try to identify three areas of interest, one of which includes this company and job. The other two should be in related fields. You've dealt with this question during the targeting phase of the search.

57. How would you define success?

Think in terms of a sense of well-being. Consider opportunity and responsibility as components of success.

58. How successful do you think you've been so far?

Say that, all-in-all, you're happy with the way your career has progressed so far. Given the normal ups and downs of life, you feel that you've done quite well and have no complaints.

Present a positive and confident picture of yourself, but don't overstate your case. An answer like, "Everything's wonderful! I can't think of a time when things were going better! I'm overjoyed!" is likely to make an interviewer wonder whether you're trying to fool him . . . or yourself. The most convincing confidence is usually quiet confidence.

"I Speak Your Language"

When we introduced this list of questions, we suggested that while it is a good idea to jot down key words or phrases as you prepare answers, it may be unwise to write out complete responses. Our point was that if you appear *too* well-prepared, you may sound mechanical or over-rehearsed in an actual interview. But there is another reason to avoid casting your answers in stone: the need to remain flexible and adaptable.

Just as no two people are exactly alike, no two interviewers are entirely similar. Each is likely to interpret your answers and assess your abilities in terms of his or her own experience and personality. In fact, trained interviewers learn that the only way to conduct objective and impartial interviews is to consider—and deal with—their own subjectivity in the process.

So while you should give careful thought and preparation to the content of your answers, you should also try to remain flexible in terms of your response to a specific interviewer's personal style.

Most of us react instinctively to obvious manifestations of personal style. If an interviewer fidgets, frowns, and looks away, we may equate his impatience with a need to get to the point and be more precise with our answers. If he looks at his watch, we're likely to assume that he has a limited amount of time to spend with us and react accordingly. If, on the other hand, he leans back in his chair, spends more than a few minutes engaging in small talk and seems in no hurry at all, then we may guess that he wants to move slowly, methodically, and intensively through the interview. We adapt to his pace. (This should not, however, be considered an invitation to ramble.)

Our reactions to style can go well beyond these responses to body language. From our earliest years—when, for instance, we may have learned that what works with a father does not work with a mother—we tailor our actions and reactions to specific situations and differing individual needs.

At Drake Beam Morin, Inc., we have developed a communications system based on a study of personal styles. We call the system "I Speak Your Language," and we have found it to be an extremely useful tool—both in job interviews and in a variety of other personal and work-related situations. It helps people understand how others act and react, both in normal circumstances and in stress conditions.

Drawn from psychological theories developed by Carl Jung, "I Speak" identifies four major personality styles which individuals use in their normal approach to work and life. Each style is associated with a main behavioral function:

STYLE	FUNCTION
Intuitor	Conceiving, projecting, inducing
Thinker	Analyzing, ordering
Feeler	Relating to experience via emotional reactions
Senser	Relating to experience through sensory perceptions

Sensers are present-oriented. They respond to things that they can feel and touch. They are the "doers" in our world.

Feelers rely on emotions, on gut feelings. They thrive on human contact and enjoy people.

Thinkers are logical, systematic, orderly, and structured. They are data-oriented.

Intuitors look to the future. They are concerned with planning and setting goals.

People tend to be blends of all four styles, and most individuals have one or two styles that are substantially better developed than the others. These are called their dominant and secondary styles. No one uses a single style in a vacuum. To place too much emphasis on one style, therefore, is to deal in stereotypes. But understanding the main styles of a person can supply fascinating clues and insights about his or her actions and reactions.

In an interview, these insights can help an individual communicate more effectively with an interviewer and make both parties feel more comfortable with each other. The interviewer has a better chance of gaining the information he seeks, and the candidate is able to present his case as effectively as possible.

As soon as you enter an interviewer's office, you can begin to look for clues to his or her communications style. First, look at the person's desk.

A *senser*'s desk is likely to be cluttered and disorderly.

A *feeler*'s desk may be covered with personal memorabilia: family photographs, vacation souvenirs, even a tennis trophy.

A *thinker*'s desk is likely to be neat and orderly. You'll probably find an electronic calculator on it.

Intuitors commonly have books and reports piled on their desks. These materials may be organized into two stacks for the purpose of comparison. Look for scholarly publications.

Next, scan the office itself.

The *senser*'s office is likely to be a mess. The floor and bookcases may be cluttered with books and reports. If there are paintings on the walls, they are likely to be action-oriented—a sailing scene, perhaps.

The *feeler*'s office is personalized. The walls may be adorned with family photos or community- and company-oriented mementoes.

The *thinker*'s surroundings are likely to be neat and simple, even sterile. Look for charts on the walls and stacks of computer printouts in the bookcase.

An *intuitor* may have abstract art on his office walls. The books in his bookcase are likely to have theoretical titles.

Third, observe the interviewer's style of dress.

Most *sensers* dress simply, but many are too busy to be very neat. Male sensers are likely to have their jackets off, their ties loosened and their shirtsleeves rolled up. Female sensers are likely to dress casually.

Feelers are extremely fashion-conscious. They favor colorful clothes. Look especially for interesting patterns in men's ties or women's outfits.

Thinkers tend to dress neatly and give careful consideration to color coordination. Men lean to traditional dark business suits. Women may wear conservative tweed suits.

Intuitors are not fashion-conscious. They may look suspiciously like the archetypal absent-minded professor. They may wear remarkably "far-out" outfits.

Fourth, look for style-clues in the interviewer's initial questions.

The *senser* is likely to get right down to business and speak about problems and their practical solutions.

The *feeler* may begin by focusing on your relationships with others or may ask whether you get personal satisfaction from your work. He or she is most likely to start the interview with a discussion of such diverse topics as family, hobbies, the weather, vacations, or new movies, and may digress at any point in the interview.

The *thinker* is interested in facts and figures. What was your college grade-point-average? How much did you save your last company?

The *intuitor* may try to relate your past to his or her future. Look for questions about your long-range goals and objectives.

Once you have a good idea of the interviewer's communications style, you can tailor your responses to meet his or her needs and expectations. For example:

Since time is of the essence to the *senser*, don't ramble. You might ask how long the interviewer has to talk with you. Expect to be interrupted by telephone calls. Be concise, candid, and factual in your answers. Stress your problem-solving abilities. Talk about getting the job done.

The *feeler* is interested in interpersonal relationships, so stress your skills and interest in working with people. Take advantage of the digressions that are likely to occur during the interview. If you find that you share a common family or community interest with the interviewer, your position may be strengthened if you mention this common ground. Feelers often seem informal or even casual in interviews. Don't assume that this makes them pushovers. They are often the most exacting interviewers of all.

The *thinker* deals in well-ordered data, so stress facts and figures in the interview with him. You might lead him step-by-step through your résumé. He is likely to seem aloof, but don't take this to mean that he is indifferent. Be specific with your answers, and avoid digressions. Don't be emotional.

In an interview with an *intuitor*, stress the future. Ask questions about company goals. Try to link your job experience to the demands of the position you are discussing. Don't dwell on the past.

Suppose, as an example, that you are in the middle of an interview and are asked the question, "Where do you see yourself going in the next two years?"

If you are talking to a *senser*, emphasize getting the current job done. "I certainly wish to grow with the company, but I think that the important thing is to get this job done properly."

Stress personal relationships with an interviewer who is a *feeler*: "My experience with people has always been fulfilling, and it makes me see myself doing . . ."

If a *thinker* asks the question, mention the past, present and future: "Based on my experience, I want to take care of this present assignment and then move on to new things."

With an *intuitor*, focus on the future: "As soon as I accomplish this immediate task, I see myself moving forward to . . ."

The "I Speak" styles are useful guides.* But don't make them a judge and jury. Any style can be used effectively or ineffectively. An intuitor may be original, or he may be unrealistic. A thinker can be prudent or gun-shy. Feelers can draw out the feelings of others, or they can stir up conflicts. Sensers may be pragmatic or shortsighted.

You must be the judge of people. If, for example, you are a senser, and you run into an intuitor in an interview, he may seem entirely too impractical, out-of-touch, or even devious for your practical, results-oriented style. If this individual is a personnel executive and you are a marketing manager the differences in your styles probably won't have long-range implications for you: The two of you would not work closely together day-in and day-out. But if the man would be your potential boss, you might worry about the chemical problems that could occur. Would you want to work with this person day after day?

Don't form an answer too quickly. The two of you might make an excellent team, as your practical qualities and his creative skills might complement each other. Many successful managers reinforce their own strong suits by attracting others whose strengths balance their own weaknesses. A creative manager may seek a detail-oriented second-in-command. An analytical thinker may avoid being too cautious by working alongside a more spontaneous feeler.

On the other hand, if you are a deliberate, prudent and rational thinker, and you decide that your potential boss is an impulsive, sentimental, and subjective feeler, you might be correct to assume that taking the job would unleash a

*We have developed a kit of "I Speak Your Language" materials: a self-administered questionnaire that lets individuals determine their own styles, a 38-page manual which explains the "I Speak" system and the four styles in detail, and a 97-page booklet of self-development exercises which allow people to sharpen their skills of identifying and dealing with the personal styles of others. The sample kit may be obtained by sending a check for $13.95 to Professional Educational Materials, A Division of Drake Beam Morin, Inc., Department A, 277 Park Avenue, New York, NY 10172.

torrent of chemical problems for you. Refuse to consider a job that places you in a no-win situation.

Careful consideration of personal communications styles can help you make these important choices. "I Speak" styles shouldn't make decisions for you, but they can help show you what to consider as you make these choices for yourself.

Practice, practice, practice. Information on personal styles and lists of questions that are likely to be asked remain theoretical tools at best until you are able to deal with all this material confidently and effectively in interview situations. You may know more about a company than its founder, you may understand your skills and goals better than your own mother, and your résumé may read like a chapter from the *Guinness Book of World Records,* but if you are not skilled at sharing the information, you won't be able to capitalize on it.

Just as actors and dancers spend long hours in rehearsal studios and athletes spend their days on practice fields, you need to prepare yourself for interviews by practicing in a realistic environment. You also need to review your preparations so that you can identify and learn from the mistakes that you are likely to make at first.

At our company, we rely heavily on videotape training to prepare our clients for interviews. Skilled counselors take the interviewer's role, engaging the client in question-and-answer sessions modeled after real interviews, and then reviewing the results, pointing out weaknesses, suggesting changes, and reinforcing effective interview techniques. If you can secure video equipment, it can be a great asset to your own interview training. You or a friend may own a home video cassette recorder, and if you do not possess a video camera, you may be able to rent one for a few days. If you cannot locate video equipment, you can certainly find an audio tape recorder and use it to preserve your answers so that you can review them following practice interviews.

You'll also need a partner to practice with, someone who is willing to play the interviewer's role. If you are acquainted with someone who is a professional interviewer, by all means ask for his or her help. Or ask your spouse or a friend for assistance.

If you approximate actual interview conditions as closely as you can in practice, you are likely to be much more relaxed and well-prepared when you get into a real interview. When the first question is asked, rather than search for words, you'll realize that you answered much the same question in a mock interview. That is an exceptionally reassuring discovery.

If you use audio equipment to record your practice interviews, ask your partner to be particularly observant of your physical appearance and reactions. Do you seem relaxed and in control of the situation, or do you appear apprehensive? Do your gestures and postures suggest that you are alert and confident, or are they disconcerting, making you look wary or unsure of yourself? Do you gesture too frequently? Do you maintain good eye contact, or does your gaze dart nervously around the room? Do you stare woodenly at the interviewer?

As the practice interview unfolds, try to conduct yourself just as you would in a real interview. Listen carefully to each question. (Many people are so concerned with answers that they never listen to the questions. It is difficult, indeed, to give a right answer by responding to the wrong question.) Don't interrupt the interviewer. Let him run the interview: That's his job. Don't blurt out your answers—take a moment to marshal your thoughts, think of key points, and then respond as clearly and concisely as you can.

When you complete a trial interview, go back through the tape to review your performance. Are you satisfied with your voice (and—if you have used videotape—with your image as well), or do you seem nervous or hesitant? If you do, additional practice will provide increased self-assurance. Do your answers sound original, or do you seem to be spewing out memorized responses? Do you speak clearly and articulately, or do you rush through your answers uncertainly?

Study the content of each response. If a question had two parts, did you remember to answer both? (Trained interviewers may ask multi-part questions to test your ability to organize yourself.) Is each answer as clear, concise, and to-the-point as you can make it? Or do you stumble around for a few sentences before getting to the heart of the question? Additional practice will help you tighten your answers.

In your answers, do you make certain to refer to your skills, accomplishments, and goals? Do you seize opportunities to make comments about your strengths and your experience without sounding like an egomaniac?

If you can, try to conduct test interviews with more than one partner. In this way, you can begin to gain experience dealing with different communications styles. As you become more familiar with your answers in successive interviews, try to polish them so that, on each occasion, you seem more alert, more original, better prepared, and more energetic than you were the last time out.

Remember that the rest of your job search doesn't stop while you are getting ready for your first selection interviews. As you continue to expand your personal contact network throughout this period, you can ask the individuals you meet for help with your interview skills. At the end of a discussion, ask for comments and suggestions about the way you handled yourself. Say that you have scheduled several important interviews for the near future and would appreciate feedback on your speaking style, mannerisms, and general interview habits.

Taking an Interview

Practice is invaluable, but it never quite duplicates the real thing. As you practice your interview methods, the following suggestions may help you improve your performance.

We've talked about the importance of doing your homework before showing up for an interview. It's even a good idea to visit the company before the day of the big event. Stop in to look things over and to check the tempo of the organization. You don't have to sneak around. Tell the receptionist that you are going to have an interview there in a few days, and ask for an annual report, recruiting brochures, or any other materials she can think of that might help you learn more about the organization. She is likely to be flattered by your interest. She'll also probably remember you favorably on the day of the interview, when the words, "Well, hello again!" can be especially comforting.

During this quick visit, look around you. How are people dressed? Are they scurrying from one place to another, or does their pace seem calm and measured? Is the reception area elaborately furnished, or is the atmosphere spartan? Is the receptionist busy, or does she seem to have time on her hands? Digesting these bits and pieces of data will help you begin to form a picture of the organization's style.

Before you leave home on the day of the interview, look yourself over carefully. Remember that everyone you meet during an interview will look very closely at you. What may be a favorite old pair of comfortable shoes to you may impress someone else as an indication that you really don't care too much about yourself. That interpretation may be entirely false, but it certainly won't help your cause.

Something that would be laughed off with someone who has spent two years proving himself a member of the team ("Hey, George, I see you're wearing one blue and one black sock today. Is that a new style?") may assume entirely different proportions in the microscopic environment of a job interview. A frayed collar or stained tie, rundown heels or unpolished shoes, a loud suit or an "un-businesslike" dress can trip you up. Wear something conservative (unless a prior visit to the firm convinces you *unequivocally* that some other style is called for). It's hard for a man—or a woman—to go astray by wearing a dark business suit.

Don't appear at the interview carrying a briefcase, suitcase, shoulderbag, and overcoat. You want to look like an alert, no-nonsense professional, not a traveling circus. Take a briefcase or attaché case if you like, but don't let excess baggage give you the posture of Willy Loman.

Arrive at least five minutes before the interview is scheduled to start. If you haven't had a chance to reconnoiter the company, the ten or fifteen minutes spent sitting in the reception area can be useful. Talk to the receptionist, if only to hear yourself speak.

If a secretary appears to usher you in to the interview, shake hands. Talk about the offices, the weather or the view. Don't be a lump. It is entirely likely that, as soon as you leave the interview, the interviewer will ask his secretary, "Well, what was your impression?" Secretaries are often their bosses' confidants. They can help your cause or knock you out of the game.

If you are offered coffee, we suggest that you politely decline until you see the interviewer with a cup in his hands. If the interviewer has coffee, accept a cup if you think it will relax you. But avoid it if you feel particularly nervous. Your hands may shake, you might spill the liquid all over yourself or, saints preserve us, all over the interviewer's desk.

Remember that it is the interviewer's job to be particularly observant. Things that might normally be overlooked will be noticed. A limp handshake or appearing five minutes late probably has never gotten anyone fired, but they have never gotten anyone hired, either.

Don't smoke. If your hands are shaking a bit, holding a cigarette will only advertise and magnify the fact. If you blow smoke in the interviewer's face, Murphy's Law of Job Selection indicates that he will turn out to be a long-distance runner who has no sense of humor about his lungs.

Body language has a great deal to do with the overall impression you make in an interview. How and where you sit can be important. Sit so that you can focus easily on the interviewer. If additional people are present, sit so that you can look at everyone without contorting yourself. Don't cut anybody out. Sit forward in your chair. That suggests eagerness and energy. Don't slouch down into a comfortable couch.

Wait for the interviewer to ask you to sit, and if you are

not sure which chair to take, ask whether the interviewer would like you to sit anywhere in particular. The interview may be conducted in an open environment, and you may walk into a room containing a round table surrounded by similar chairs. Don't just drop yourself down: Murphy's Second Law of Job Selection indicates that you will have chosen the interviewer's favorite chair.

Look around the office. If you see personal items, mention them. If there is a boat model on a table, for example, ask about it. If pictures of children adorn the walls, ask about them. Try to determine whether you and the interviewer share things in common that you might chat about for a minute or two. If, by contrast, the office is decorated with a calculator and stacks of computer printouts, prepare yourself to get right down to business.

Be positive from the start. Don't begin by saying that the weather certainly is lousy today or by wondering aloud why the buses never run on time. We've seen people walk into an office for the first time and say, "Gee, what an ugly plant!" Remember that you are "on stage" every minute of an interview. You need to get passing grades throughout the meeting.

Try to build a sense of rapport with the interviewer right from the start. Help set the positive tone that is characteristic of good interviews by being alert, energetic, and outgoing.

Finally, remember that no matter how well you have prepared yourself, you must let the interviewer lead the discussion. People who say, "I really took that interview over and turned it around," are usually only boasting. Don't wrestle for control.

If you run into a poorly trained interviewer (and, sooner or later, you will), you'll simply have to live with the situation and do whatever you can to make the interview work. He's the only interviewer you have at that moment, and however dismal a job he does, he can probably still see to it that you never get any further at that organization. Work with him, not against him. If, for example, the interviewer spends most of the time talking about the company, he has not prepared himself to conduct a proper selection interview. The best you can do is to show that you are knowledgeable and enthusiastic about the organization. Ask questions about the outfit. You want that person to leave the interview thinking good thoughts about you.

As the questions begin, remember to be a good listener. First, make sure that you've heard the question correctly. If a question isn't clear, ask for clarification. Don't simply jump in and embarrass yourself by answering a question that wasn't asked. If you can't answer a question, say so.

Respond directly to the question and only to that question. Don't volunteer information unless it is both positive and pertinent to the question that has just been asked.

Avoid using key material about yourself to answer the first few questions. It may take the interviewer a few minutes to settle down and focus his concentration fully on you and your accomplishments. Save your "big guns" for a few minutes later in the discussion.

Above all else, be brief. If you find that you are talking in six- or seven-minute stretches, bells and whistles should go off in your mind. If the interviewer wants to know more about a subject than you have offered, he'll ask for elaboration. Or, if you give a concise answer but wonder if you have, in fact, satisfied the interviewer, ask him if your answer covers the subject or if you should give additional details. Make it clear that you want to answer each question fully but do not want to bore the interviewer.

Don't head too far in the other direction, however. If your responses consist of a single syllable, or if the interviewer asks you to elaborate every question, then you should spend a bit more time on your answers.

While it is the interviewer's responsibility to lead the discussion, it is your job to make certain that you present yourself well. Weave strengths and accomplishments into your answers. Be positive about everything you say. Show the interviewer that you've done your homework on the company. But don't run off at the mouth.

There may be some subjects that you must raise yourself. For example, we counseled one man who walked with the aid of crutches. On the day before he was to travel to Washington, D.C., for an important job interview, we went through a mock interview with him. After about five minutes of questions, we stopped and asked how he thought he was doing. He believed that things were going well. We agreed that he was certainly answering the questions nicely but said that the interview wasn't going well at all.

Our point had to do with his crutches. Here was an obvious physical consideration that no one would miss, that many interviewers would not bring up, and that would make everyone wonder, "Can this man do the job?" We told our client that he should make it his responsibility to raise and answer that question.

Shortly after the real interview began, our client said to the interviewer, "I feel that I should say a word or two about these crutches. I can tell you that I woke up at home this morning, got to the airport on time, flew to Washington, took a cab from the airport to your offices, and arrived five minutes early." He also got the job.

If, for instance, you walk into an interview and the interviewer realizes for the first time that you are about 62 years old, you'd better deal with the issue. He can't ask you about your age without breaking a ton of laws. But don't imagine that he won't think about it. Meet the question head-on by talking about your experience and track record.

Toward the end of the interview, you'll probably be asked if you have any questions about the job or the organization. If anything important has been left out of the discussion, here is where you can bring up the subject.

You should also be prepared with several questions for the interviewer. But give them some thought. If you are talking to a would-be boss, for instance, and have spent the past hour convincing him of your interest in the job and the excitement and opportunity it seems to offer, don't finish by asking about health benefits or pension plans. He may leave the interview wondering whether you're more interested in getting the job done or in your personal security. If you are speaking with a personnel executive, however, these can be valid questions. But identify them as details, not as burning central issues.

Here are some general questions to guide your thinking as you prepare your own:

- What are some of the more important objectives that you would like to see accomplished on this job?
- What is most pressing? What would you like to have done in the next two or three months?
- What freedom would I have to determine my own work objectives, deadlines and methods of measurement?
- What are some of the most difficult problems that someone would face in this position? How do you think these could be best handled?
- What might be some possible sources of dissatisfaction?
- How would you describe your (or my future supervisor's) management style?
- How does this compare with your (or his) boss and those above him or her, particularly the organization's chief executive?
- Where could a person go in the organization who is successful in this position? Within what time frame?

At the conclusion of the interview, make sure to find out what your next step should be. Will someone contact you? Should you make an appointment to talk with someone else in the organization? When might you expect to hear something? Should you provide any additional materials or infor-

mation? Be sure to thank the interviewer for his or her time
and interest.

After the interview, you may be able to take some action
to further your cause without appearing too anxious or seeming to meddle. You should certainly send the interviewer a
short thank-you note. If an important point comes to mind
following the interview which you think should have been
mentioned, you might raise it in this letter. You could also
suggest that appropriate references be contacted.

You should also critique your performance while the details of the interview remain fresh in your mind. Were you
relaxed but alert? Were you well enough prepared so that
your answers were clear without seeming rehearsed? Were
you surprised by any of the questions? Did you ramble or
were your answers concise and to the point? Overall, how did
you feel about your peformance? You'll undoubtedly find
ways to improve your presentation for future interviews.

8 * "Nothing's Working!"

FINDING a job and reading a book about finding a job are not the same thing at all. In books, topics can be arranged, manipulated, and introduced so that one subject follows another swiftly and, it seems, logically. Things never seem to be quite so well-ordered in real life.

Suppose that you are two months into your job search. The first month wasn't bad. Perhaps because you couldn't have felt much worse immediately after you lost your job, your spirits generally improved during the first five or six weeks. You had straightforward, mechanical things to do: putting a résumé together, producing a mailing, answering want ads. You began to feel hopeful as you started to receive encouraging responses about your campaign.

Then all of a sudden, you realize that nine or ten weeks have passed since you lost your job, and nothing meaningful seems to be happening. Your mailbox has filled up with rejection letters from fifty-nine of the sixty companies contacted. You haven't heard a word from 98% of the search firms you approached. A close friend doesn't return a telephone call. You meet with an executive who spends forty-five minutes tearing into your résumé. In the middle of an interview, an executive from one of the few search firms that did get in touch with you announces, "I'm not so sure that you're in the right field at all." Things seem shaky, and you may begin to doubt your plans and yourself. You land one or two actual job interviews, but nothing comes of them. Perhaps you should quit the rat-race entirely and open a ski lodge in Wyoming or start a sailboat charter business in the Caribbean. You feel alone and forgotten. "I guess I really don't have any friends," you think. "The people I counted on certainly didn't come through."

You begin to doubt your résumé, so you rewrite it, hoping that a different document might work some new magic. You abandon your contact network and withdraw into yourself. You ask yourself a question that you thought you had answered affirmatively weeks ago: "Am I ever going to find another job?"

You will, if you stick to your plan. Almost any job search—like virtually anything else in life—is a series of peaks and valleys. Most peoples' lives are successions of good times and difficult times. Why should looking for a job be any different?

It's perfectly normal to receive one or two leads for every 100 letters you mail. That is the expected response rate, so you are not being realistic—or fair with yourself—if you consider it an unacceptable return. You ought to expect that 95% or 97% or even 100% of the search firms you contact won't have anything for you at any given time. Your personal contacts will dry up from time to time. It isn't that they don't like you or haven't been thinking about you. It's that they don't have anything for you. They look around and find that they don't have a job to offer you and can't think of anyone else to send you to see.

The thing that will pull you through such hard times is perseverance. When you keep plugging away, something surfaces, often where you least expect it. Two or three important doors open, and your whole campaign picks up. This cycle, incidentally, may repeat itself two or three times during the course of your job search. When you find the right job, of course, you reach a new peak. But even that doesn't last forever, as you jump to the new set of highs and lows that are a normal part of any job.

It's easy for us to deliver a "Stick to it" sermon, and it may be very difficult for you to accept the message, particularly if it comes at a point in your job search when you feel worried or demoralized.

But giving in to the situation can be dangerous. If you decide that your search won't work, that you'll never find a job, or that you may as well give up, you may wind up digging a very deep hole for yourself. We feel that the best way out of this dilemma is to stick with your plan and get back to the basics of your job search.

Go to the library and look up new companies to contact. Get back to work on your personal contact network. Check back with the people you've already talked with, not to cry on their shoulders but to tell them how you are progressing and to let them know that you are still available. You might start these conversations by saying that you have a number of plans going, that your investigations have prompted you to alter your thinking somewhat, and that, as a result, you are now heading in a direction that is somewhat different than the one you last talked about.

Look through the rejection letters you received when you sent out a mailing to companies. Call the individuals who signed the letters and talk to them about their companies. The results may amaze you. Most people will admire your tenacity and appreciate the fact that you are sufficiently interested in their company to get in touch with them. And the employment situation may have changed at that organization.

If you sent a résumé and cover letter to fifteen or thirty search firms, mail materials to forty or sixty or one hundred more (see chapter 6). If more than two months have passed since your first mailing, send another package to the search organizations you've already contacted. Many will have discarded your résumé as soon as they determined that they had no immediate openings that corresponded to your skills and experience. And even the largest firms with the most sophisticated filing systems often throw out résumés after three months because they assume that the documents are no longer up-to-date.

Don't assume that any organization is so efficient that it either *knows* it is not interested in you or is sufficiently impressed by your credentials to keep your résumé on file. Your materials may have been lost, misrouted, or never returned to someone who passed them along to an associate for comment.

Don't suppose that you've been forgotten, but at the same time, don't imagine that everyone remembers you, either. Jog memories. Realize that it's your responsibility to keep yourself visible.

We believe that for at least the first six months of your search, it is much wiser to stay with your original plan than to tamper with it or change your program drastically. If things still don't seem to be working at the end of six months, then it's time to reassess and perhaps fine-tune your plan. But don't scrap it. Review your program by examining the way you've implemented it.

Are you maintaining regular monthly contact with fifty members of your network? Do you check in with an additional fifty people every two months? Are you answering an average of three newspaper or trade journal advertisements each week? Have you sent a direct mailing to 100 companies? Have you contacted 150 search firms? If you haven't maintained this level of activity through the first six months of your job search, then it is highly likely that it's execution—not planning—that needs to be improved.

If, after eight or nine months, your search seems seriously stalled, then you should go back and reassess your plan. Are you perhaps one job away from the job you really want? Should you consider accepting free-lance or consulting work on a project basis to get you through this difficult period without getting locked into an undesirable job? Have you limited your search unnecessarily by identifying your needs

too precisely? For example, is geographical location as important to you now as it was eight months ago? By doubling the
area in which you would be willing to work, you might markedly increase your chances of finding the job that's been elud-
ing you.

We counseled one man who had been the president of a
major consumer corporation. For months he worked his plan
diligently but continued to finish second in one search after
another. Finally we encouraged him to accept a job that was
obviously a bit below his needs and abilities. We thought it
would help him survive emotionally and weather the dol-
drums he seemed unable to escape. We urged him to take
the job and continue his search. He didn't shut down his
contact network, and, within a few months, he found another
position that fit his skills and experience perfectly.

That was an extreme situation, however, and we would
certainly counsel anyone to think long and hard before making such a decision. Don't settle for just any job if you've
been out of work for three or four or even six months. If
economic conditions make waiting for the right job an impossible luxury, then you'll obviously have to consider interim
employment. But hold onto your plan for as long as you can.
Give it time to work.

We know one man who lost his job with a large, sophisticated company, sat for three months without doing a thing,
and then, with no thought or planning, took the first job that
was offered to him. He lasted six months in the new job,
where even a cursory investigation would have alerted him to
the obvious and serious chemical problems that he did, in
fact, encounter as soon as he joined the company. When he
was fired for the second time in less than a year, his spirits
were understandably low. He became even more panicked
than he had been the first time around, refused help, and
landed in a trap from which he may never extricate himself.
It is probably impossible to overemphasize the importance of
planning.

Outside support may help when things aren't going well.
One man talked with his minister, who told him, "You know,

it seems that a lot of people are out of work right now." The message was hardly a revelation, but it did boost the man's spirits. It helped to know that he wasn't alone in his predicament.

Many churches and community organizations run programs for people who are looking for jobs. These can help in two ways. First, sharing experiences and fears with others can be very reassuring. At our company, the informal support and friendship that our clients give one another have proved to be potent tools in their searches.

Second, these informal groups often become clearinghouses for specific details about the mechanical aspects of the job search. One member points another to a new contact or search firm.

We don't suggest that you look to these groups for real vocational counseling, however. Don't let a well-meaning acquaintance shape your future for you. If, at this stage, you aren't comfortable with your own plans, contact a professional counselor for help.

We've watched thousands of our clients find new jobs. We've worked with people who are geniuses and individuals who are not. We've counseled men and women with serious physical and psychological problems. Through all this, we've discovered that the ease or difficulty with which all of them find jobs is usually linked to their willingness to accept the premise that searching for work is a systematic process. The people who stick to that process find jobs most easily. No matter how intelligent or experienced or energetic they may be, the individuals who either do not make plans or will not stay with them have the most trouble finding good jobs.

You can't control the process. Timing has too much to do with finding a job: A position must be available for you to take it, and you must be aware of it to find it. But by pursuing your plan relentlessly, by adding layer upon layer of individuals who know that you are skilled and available, you can expand your search universe so that you affect the process and ultimately succeed at finding an exciting, satisfying job.

9 * Negotiating an Offer

IF the selection interview is the most important event in the process of finding a new job, negotiating an offer can be the most delicate. You reach a critical stage in your search when you realize that a prospective employer is serious about wanting to hire you. Until this happens, you're most likely to present yourself in terms of what you can offer the employer. But when the employer indicates his interest in hiring you, you should be ready to discuss the things you need in return. Most people find that it is far easier to say, "Here's what I'd like to do for you," than to assert, "Here's what I'd like you to do for me."

You have every right to expect reasonable rewards for the work you will do and the responsibilities you will accept in a new job. Still, determining what these rewards should be, and reaching agreement with an employer about them, often seems to be an undertaking of heroic proportions.

The negotiating process sometimes turns out to be simple and straightforward. You may receive an offer that exceeds your expectations for a job that more than meets your needs. Your response is likely to be a quick, "When do I start?"

Should this occur, incidentally, don't fall for the "That

was too easy, why didn't I ask for more, I should kick myself"
game. The point of negotiating an offer is not to break the
bank but to strike a deal that satisfies you and the company.
If you reach that point in the first round of negotiations, so
much the better. You should feel secure knowing how well-
attuned you and your new associates are to each other.

But when you consider how many variables can be involved, it seems likely that you and your prospective employer will have to discuss the terms of the deal in some
detail so that everyone will be comfortable with the situation.

Money is the most obvious consideration. On the subject of compensation alone, you may need to think about
such items as bonuses, health and life insurance coverage, a
pension or annuity, a profit-sharing plan, an expense account,
a club membership, a company car, a relocation allowance, a
stock option plan, or some other incentive program.

Important negotiable areas may not be related to fi-
nances. You could find it necessary to settle questions about
your title or job responsibilities. You may need to discuss the
size and composition of your staff. You may want to inquire
about an employment contract. You may wish to talk about
where you will fit into the company's organizational plan.
You might want to discuss technical support: computers or
telecommunications systems, say, that you think you'll need
to succeed at the job.

You may even have to negotiate things *out* of the job,
that is, refuse to take on duties that really don't fit your
professional skills, for instance, or responsibilities that aren't
in line with your personal needs.

Making a Checklist

Since negotiating is such a specialized, particular process, it
might make sense to actually write out a list of negotiable
concerns that you think you should raise, and bring the docu-

ment into the negotiating session. At the end of the discussion, you might even leave a copy with the company representative so that he is clear about the territory you have covered. The list of topics might include (but need not be limited to):

> Salary
> Bonus
> Stock option
> Company incentive program
> Deferred compensation
> Life insurance
> Health coverage
> Pension or annuity
> Profit-sharing plan
> Expense account
> Company car
> Club membership
> Relocation allowance
> Title
> Job responsibilities
> Staff
> Support structure
> Employment contract

The Basic Principle of Negotiating

You can simplify the process of understanding and resolving these matters by realizing that the key to effective negotiating—call it the basic principle of negotiating—is to link each negotiable item to the job itself. How does it relate to the job? How might it affect your ability to perform the job effectively? How will it affect your satisfaction with the position and the company?

Suppose that you are trying to determine the title you should hold. You want to join the company as a vice president. Ask yourself why.

If you want to be a vice president simply because you've always liked the title and think that now would be a good time to have it, you are on thin negotiating ice. But suppose you want to be a vice president because you realize that you'll spend most of your time dealing with other vice presidents and think you can perform your job best by approaching them with corporate status similar to their own. Then you have an acceptable, performance-related reason to raise the issue. If being a vice president makes you more effective, it serves the job and may make sense to the company. If it only makes you look or feel better, it isn't a legitimate negotiating concern.

Suppose you decide that you want a certain salary because you believe that an individual with your background doing this job at this company in this industry deserves this level of compensation. You are thinking reasonably. That doesn't mean that the company will necessarily agree with you, but you certainly have a legitimate negotiable concern. If you want a certain salary because you'd like to buy a bigger house or a smaller car, you are probably not on solid ground.

The Importance of Timing

As soon as you sense that you are "getting warm" with a company, you'll probably begin to think about these subjects. But you shouldn't raise them until an appropriate moment arises. Good timing, in fact, is crucial to good negotiating.

Don't move too quickly. Making a demand—or even airing a suggestion—before an employer has decided that he or she really wants you to join the organization is particularly dangerous.

Suppose you say, "I'd really like to come in at $50,000 a year." On one day, a potential employer might think, "What is wrong with this person? I don't know if I want to hire him, and he's telling me how much he wants to be paid."

On the next day, his reaction might be, "Well, I am leaning toward this person, but I haven't entirely ruled out my second choice, either. And I did set a $47,000 ceiling on this job. Maybe I should think some more about the other guy."

Had you waited another day, the employer might have decided, "Well, I've made up my mind: I want this person on board. If that costs me another $3,000, it's a worthwhile investment."

If you negotiate too soon, you can decrease an employer's interest. If you wait until a clear interest to hire you appears, you've shifted the focus. The employer may now feel an increased need to bargain with you.

How do you tell when the time is ripe to negotiate? If you are asked to return to a company for successive rounds of interviews, you're getting warm. If you seem to be talking with decision-makers on these occasions, you're drawing closer. When you hear a definite expression of interest from a company representative, you ought to be prepared to negotiate.

The tip-off might be a comment like, "We really are interested in you. What kinds of concerns do you have about us? We'd really like to see whether we can get closer to a final decision." Or the signal may be more direct. "What's it going to take to get you to come with us?" you could be asked. Obviously, it's your move.

Don't wait too long to make that move. You cannot make a final decision about a job—whether it's the right position for you—until you understand the details and conditions that surround it. As a result, you obviously need to deal with all negotiable items before accepting or rejecting an offer. If you accept a job and then turn around and say, "By the way, do you think you could throw in a country-club membership, too?" your request will probably be met with a cool stare. You will not have enhanced your stature with the company you have just joined. Had you asked the question earlier, the most negative reaction you'd have risked could have been, "Nice try." Ask too late, and you invite an entirely different response: "Who does this guy think he is?"

If trying to negotiate after you have accepted an offer is ill-advised, attempting to negotiate after you start work makes even less sense. Suppose that, on your second day of work, having decided that you should have asked for an additional $5,000 in salary, you bring the issue to your boss's attention. You are no longer negotiating your salary; you are now asking for a raise. Even if your superiors think that you deserve an increase after sixteen hours on the job, they probably won't be able to give it to you without setting a dangerous precedent for the rest of the company. They are more likely to wonder why they hired you in the first place, and that is not an auspicious beginning to a new job.

Or suppose you say, after your first month at work, "You know, on my last job I had a company car, and I never realized how valuable it was until now. What are my chances of getting a car here?"

The reply might be, "Sorry, but we have a firm policy on that: no company cars." Had you thought to raise the issue before you accepted an offer from the company, you could have continued the discussion: "O.K., if that's company policy, I understand. But I figure that my car was worth $3,000 a year in income. Can you work with me on my salary to adjust for that?" You might not have gotten your wish, but you would at least have raised the issue in an acceptable context, and you would have had an answer before you accepted the job.

Preparing to Negotiate

However important timing may be, knowing when to speak up is half the battle at best—and probably much less. To negotiate successfully, you obviously have to know *what* to say as well. This calls for careful preparation.

What topics should you stress as you try to reach agreement on an offer? What subjects are less important to you? Should you be rigid or flexible in your demands? What is the cut-off between an agreement that satisfies you and one that does not?

To answer these questions, you need to review the target you created during the planning and organizing phase of your search, you need to think about the specific details of the job you are now considering, and you need to compare the two.

Think back to the targeting process. As you planned your job search, you focused your campaign by identifying the things that make a job valuable and satisfying for you. After assessing your career accomplishments, your skills and your needs for the future, you drew a rather precise target for your search. At its center was a hypothetical position that met all your personal and professional needs—a "dream" job. As you moved out from the bull's-eye, you encountered employment territory which, while being somewhat less than perfect, was still acceptable to you. Enough of your needs would be sufficiently well taken care of by jobs landing in this terrain to make them worthwhile. At the edge of the target, the least acceptable jobs would be located. Positions that offered anything less would be unacceptable to you and would miss the target entirely.

By rating a specific offer in terms of the values that you think are important, you can determine whether it hits or misses your target. If it hits the target, you can see how close to the bull's-eye it lands. If it misses entirely, you can decide whether, by negotiating additional items into the job, you might be able to improve it enough to move it to within the limits of your target.

If you refer back to chapter 4, you'll find a chart on which you ranked the importance of a number of variables in terms of your needs. Now, by using the information you've gained from research and interviews, you can rate a specific job in terms of these same variables. Some of the values you assign may be unsubstantiated just yet. You can certainly be precise in rating the organization's size, for instance, but as you consider an item like compensation base, you may have to rely on an educated guess unless a firm salary figure has already been established. As you move through the negotiating process, you can verify these estimates and, if need be, alter your impression of the situation accordingly. But you need to start someplace, and you can at least begin the process by thinking in terms of the best knowledge that is presently available to you.

For the sake of simplicity, consider this short version of the chart, which accounts for only three variables:

CRITERIA	My Needs	Company A		Company B		Company C	
	(1)	(2)	(1)x(2)	(3)	(1)x(3)	(4)	(1)x(4)
Decision-making Authority	6	9					
Size of Company	7	4					
Compensation base	8	9					
TOTAL SCORES							

At this point in the deliberative process, incidentally, you don't need to multiply your needs by Company A's values. That becomes useful when you have more than one offer to consider, since it gives you a numerical system to weigh and compare each in relation to your needs. Right now, you want to consider a single job in terms of the things that are important to you.

Start by looking at non-negotiable items—company size, for example. (It is unlikely that you are going to be able to do anything about the size of a company, so that can be considered a non-negotiable item.) You cannot alter a non-negotiable item, so if it makes a job unacceptable, you have no choice but to turn down the offer. You may as well find that out before negotiating anything.

By assigning it a value of 7, the individual described in our example indicated that company size is important to him, but not absolutely critical. There is a meaningful discrepancy between his needs in this area and the situation he has encountered at Company A. Perhaps he wants the flexibility of a very small organization, and Company A is a medium-sized firm. This individual needs to decide whether the difference is great enough to make the job unacceptable, or whether other variables might tilt the scale back in favor of accepting an offer.

Suppose he had assigned a value of 10 to company size, and Company A earned a 2 in that category, a situation that might occur if an individual who was convinced that he needed a very small organization to enjoy and succeed at his job was offered employment at an ITT or IBM. No matter how greatly other considerations might sweeten the offer, it would probably be foolish for such an individual to accept a position at a place that is so at odds with his own needs.

People frequently consider these non-negotiable topics in much less deliberate, but no less effective, fashion. If you walk out of an interview telling yourself, "No way on earth I'd work for people like that," you've gone through exactly the same process, perhaps deciding that the organization's management style, which you would be unlikely to change, is entirely at odds with your own needs.

It is absolutely critical to deal with these issues honestly and not let negotiable considerations blur their importance. Many people get themselves into real employment trouble by accepting jobs that are basically and irrevocably wrong for them. Usually they decide that some negotiated item will compensate for the position's underlying and unalterable shortcomings.

This occurs most frequently when substantial amounts of money prompt people to ignore their better judgment and accept positions for which they are ill-suited or ill-qualified. A statement like, "For that kind of money, I'll do whatever they want," or a thought like, "At that salary, I'll learn how

to do the job," is a tip-off to this perilous situation. People
who take jobs hoping that financial incentives will make
them bearable learn with depressing regularity and terrible
clarity that such is frequently not the case.

But to return to our illustration, let us assume that the
difference between the two numbers is not great enough to
make this individual categorically reject an offer on the basis
of company size alone.

He moves on to negotiable variables. Here, the first is
decision-making authority. He has rated himself with a 6.
The ability to make decisions is important to him, but certainly not an overriding employment factor. The position he
is considering ranks very highly in this area, earning a 9. Our
man would apparently be in a position to make many decisions if he took this job.

At first glance, it appears that, in this regard, the job
more than meets his needs. And that may be the case. If he
needs a certain amount of decision-making power to be satisfied, *and would not mind having more*, all is well. But if he
really does not want to have too much authority, if he is
uncomfortable when he has to make too many decisions, for
instance, or if he doesn't deal well with the stress of reaching
particularly important decisions, then the disparity between
his own needs and the job's requirements might be significant.

The final variable in our example is base compensation, and here things look fine. The individual believes that
this job would come with a salary somewhat higher than the
figure he has determined is necessary for him. There is a
possibility that too much salary might bring adverse tax implications, and the individual might think about trying to
negotiate some other, non-taxable benefits in exchange for a
certain amount of starting salary. Dealing with an embarrassment of riches is usually considered a nice problem.

If these were the only criteria involved in the situation,
our individual might take the data and reason this way:

"There seems to be somewhat more decision-making here than I had been looking for, but I feel comfortable enough with my ability to handle the additional load, and the higher salary is an acceptable reward for the added work and responsibility. The company is a bit larger than I ideally wanted, but it's not too big. If this is, in fact, what I'm offered, I think I'll take the job."

On the other hand, he might have concluded, "The job pays exceptionally well, but the company seems too big for me. And I know myself well enough to understand that I feel most comfortable implementing other people's decisions, not making them myself. The responsibility for making so many important decisions would really get to be a burden. I'd better keep looking."

In real life, of course, the decision would have been much more complex, because there would have been additional variables to consider. But the example does show how important it is to know both your own needs and all the details of an offer in order to reach a good decision about taking or refusing a job.

As you prepare your own negotiating position, then, your deliberations should include as many variables as you can come up with. You might start with your last job. What were the conditions of employment there? Should there be different arrangements here? Do you deserve the same employment package? If you've made a career change, you may not. Do you deserve more? The act of taking a new job is not automatic grounds for a raise. But if the new job involves increased responsibilities, perhaps you should receive more for your efforts.

You need to do as much homework as you can. Is there some way to learn what the position you are interviewing for is worth at this company? If a search firm has been involved, its representative should be able to help. Is the industry as a whole considered high- or low-paying? Does the specific company have a reputation for generosity or stinginess? Is it known for comprehensive benefit packages? Does it have an incentive plan which rewards exceptional performance? If it does, what determines an individual's eligibility for it?

The more information you possess at the outset, the better prepared you will be to negotiate an acceptable deal for yourself, because you will be less likely to be surprised by subjects you didn't anticipate.

When you have considered as many variables as you can think of, from job title to vacation policy, you should also think about the flexibility with which you can negotiate. This varies from job to job and is linked to your target. If the job is at or near the center of your target, you can afford to be extremely flexible as you negotiate. You are looking at something that is close to an "I'd give anything for that job" situation, and, while you probably wouldn't give *anything*, you can afford to be generous. The job will still offer enough positive qualities to make it fall well within the limits of your search plan.

As you consider jobs that are somewhat farther away from the bull's-eye, you have less to bargain with. When you reach the edge of your target, giving away anything might make the offer unacceptable. Finally, if you are trying to salvage a position that does not land inside your target now, you have nothing to barter away, and, in fact, the company must agree to make concessions to you if you are to accept the offer.

The more flexible you can be, of course, the more likely you are to reach agreement. Negotiating is a process of compromise, after all. But your first duty is to find a job that is the right job for you. If you take too little, or give up too much, you'll have spent a remarkable amount of time and energy finding the wrong job. The better prepared you are at the beginning of the negotiating process, the better able you'll be to avoid that catastrophic turn of events.

The Negotiating Process

You've done your homework and made your preparations. You know what an ideal offer would involve, and you know what you can accept and still be satisfied. Your potential employer has given you a clear signal that it is time to negotiate. What do you do now?

First, relax a bit. For most of us, simply mentioning the word "negotiate" raises images of adversaries arguing about the shapes of conference tables. That probably won't be your fate. (And if it is, you should wonder whether you really want to make a career of spending your days with people like that.) It is more likely that you've located both a job that you want very much and an employer who wants you very much. The two of you do need to reach agreement about a number of things, but you'll begin the process from this very positive point of departure.

Reaching agreement may call for compromise. Still, if you have to give a little (a fringe benefit that you were originally interested in, or even a certain amount of starting salary, for instance) to gain a great deal (a job that you will find rewarding and satisfying) the net result will be a substantial gain. As we've said, you do have to set limits to your generosity to avoid landing yourself in an unacceptable job, but as long as you know these limits, and until you bump into them, think of negotiating in terms of two parties aiming for the same goal.

Perhaps the employer will open the discussion by asking, "Well, just what would you need from us to join the company?" He is probably thinking about dollars, but you may wish to preface your remarks with a more general statement.

"Before we get into details," you might say, "it might make sense for me to review my understanding of the position. Several things seem very clear: You're looking for a marketing vice president, who will report directly to you, who will manage a staff of about twenty-five people and a budget of $19 million, and who will be responsible for all the marketing-related activities of this division.

"Other things may be assumptions on my part, but, based on the discussions I've had here, I believe that you see two immediate priorities for this individual: getting two new products—both of which are now behind schedule—into the marketplace, and beginning to strengthen the marketing staff so that similar delays won't disrupt future plans. In the long term, I think that you are most interested in strengthening the R&D functions of the department to bolster planning efforts. Those are exactly the kinds of challenges I'm looking for, so I hope that this is a fair assessment of the situation."

You should get quick agreement from the employer. If you don't, you may have a problem. You certainly can't negotiate if you are talking about one job and he or she is discussing another. But at this stage in the selection process, that would be highly unlikely.

You've done several things with this statement. First, you've opened the discussion with a subject that you are both almost certain to agree on. That's a good positive start. Second, you've tied the entire negotiating discussion to the job itself. You've mentioned what needs to be done, and you've indicated how greatly you want to do it.

Now you can approach the thorny subject of compensation. You might begin by saying, "I'm as interested in money as anyone else, I suppose, but I am more interested in this job. I know I can do it. So my primary concern is getting the opportunity to get in and prove myself. If I do, I'm sure that the dollars will take care of themselves." This statement links financial considerations to performance-related job issues.

In general, people who are more concerned with the work they do than with side issues—salary included—are people who do their work best and are happiest in their jobs. Companies are interested in how well the work is done, naturally, and so they like to be convinced that the job, not the paycheck, is uppermost in a candidate's mind. Individuals, in addition, should certainly be interested in how happy they are with their jobs.

We believe that this is the way things should be. The whole point of this book and the system it describes is to help people put themselves into jobs that make them happy, satisfied, and successful. We find, incidentally, that when people *are* genuinely gripped by their work, they do it well, and the dollars really *do* take care of themselves. If you find yourself worrying more about what the job will pay than about what it will do for you as an individual, perhaps you should reconsider the position.

You certainly don't want to give the impression that you care less about the job than about what it will get you, and you do want to be sure that you don't make a prospective employer think that you are looking for financial ways to make the position attractive enough to accept. But it is equally risky to avoid the topic or to undersell yourself. You can't say, "Well, I'm not sure what I'm worth, what do you think?" You can't agree to accept a job at any level, and you don't want to suggest that you don't know your own worth.

Here is where the importance of good preparation becomes so obvious. You should have both a salary goal and a lowest acceptable figure in mind, and you should be able to tie your goal to your own experience and to the demands of the job.

If your research has shown that there is a definite salary range for the job, you might say, "As I understand it, this job pays between $52,000 and $56,000 at your company. I would find the top figure in that range acceptable. That's about ten percent more than I earned at my previous job, but I think that the added responsibility of this position more than accounts for the difference."

If there is no salary range, it's usually best to fall back on your past compensation history: "I was earning $51,000 when I left my previous position," you might say, "and like anyone else, I'd like a bump. Given that natural inclination, and, more specifically, considering the additional demands of this position, I'd like a ten percent increase over that figure."

If the company representative says, "No problem," you can move on to the next topic. (And don't kick yourself. You got what you asked for. Don't get tricky and try to ask for more.)

But suppose he does not agree. The most important thing is this: Don't get stuck this early in the negotiations. Let the employer's response dictate your reaction. If he says, "I'm not sure I can quite match that, but we shouldn't be too far away from each other," don't belabor the subject. Say something like, "Fine. Let's move on to some other concerns, and perhaps they'll help us agree on the exact salary figure." You might even say, "That sounds fine to me. If we agree on an overall package, I don't want to argue about a couple of thousand dollars."

Suppose your would-be boss' reaction is, "Whew, I think we may have a real problem here. I don't think I can get anywhere near that figure." Don't get rigid or defensive or give up on the job. Probe a bit: "Well, how far apart are we?" Say that he tells you that he had planned to offer no more than $40,000 for the position. You might reply, "That certainly is a problem, but this certainly is the job I want, too. Let's put salary aside for the moment and see if there are some other areas where we can make up the difference." There is no way that you are going to get a $16,000 salary concession at this early stage of the game, so move to another topic for now.

You could, after all, be pleasantly surprised later in the discussion. You might say, "I'd like to know whether we could choose some way to measure my performance on the job and link an appropriate bonus system to it." The company representative might answer, "You mean that no one told you about our bonus plan? Why, it's averaged 42% of annual base salary in each of the last four years."

Or you might be able to make up the difference in increments: A company car that you hadn't expected could be worth a certain amount to you, a club membership so much more, and the discovery that the company's medical plan includes full dental coverage for your family might offset the loss of untold thousands of pre-tax salary dollars if you have two children with peculiar bites and expensive orthodonture bills.

Suppose that at the end of your talk, you feel you've found $9,000 in additional benefits. That would leave you, at most, $7,000 away from your original salary goal. (The difference might actually be less if the tax implications of benefits versus taxable salary dollars are considered.) You could say, "The only problem I see is that question of salary. Do you think we could split the difference? I could live with $48,000 to start. It's actually less than my previous salary, but the benefits here are somewhat better than I'd anticipated, and I do want this job. I think I'll be able to make up the difference pretty rapidly once I get to work here."

The employer might answer, "That would still create real problems in terms of internal salary parity. I think the best I could stretch it to would be $46,000."

Added to your $9,000 of found benefits, you would only be $1,000 away from your original salary goal. That's a small price to pay for a satisfying job. In addition, you would have impressed your boss that you are exceptionally reasonable and that you are determined to have that job.

Starting salary is important, however, particularly since many raises are figured on percentages. If you join a company at a high level, you get large-dollar-amount raises. It is more difficult to make this sort of headway after you join a company, because your percentage increase is likely to be tied to those of the people around you.

You could try to build an earlier-than-normal review into your agreement if you cannot get together on salary. "If that's the best we can do, I'll settle for it," you might say, "but do you think we could move the first review date up to three months from now?"

"That's too short a time," the employer might answer.

"What about doing it at six months?"

"Fine," you say.

The key to all this is to remain as flexible as you can for as long as you are able. Don't be in a hurry to throw in the towel unless you realize that there is something fundamentally and irreparably wrong with the job.

Ultimately, you are the only one who can really know the best direction to take in salary negotiations. The characteristics of particular offers multiplied by the diversity of individual needs indicates that no two negotiating situations will be precisely alike.

You might even encounter a situation in which the problem is too much salary, not too little. We counseled one man who was in the running for a job as vice president of marketing with a major corporation. Our client had been earning about $50,000 a year in his previous job, and the position for which he was being considered had a $100,000 price tag attached to it. The employer had narrowed his search to two candidates: our client and another individual who was making $80,000 and was in his late 40s. (Our man was in his late 30s.)

The company was close to a decision, and the momentum seemed to be shifting in the direction of the other candidate. Their reason was apparently that his last salary, and perhaps his age, made him seem the more likely candidate. The company developed an informal ability quotient, making a connection between his salary, his age, and the new job. They began to wonder how our client, making $50,000 a year, could be ready to step into a $100,000 job, even though he had already impressed them enough with his experience, energy, and skills to reach the final round of the search.

Our client dealt with the problem by fitting his negotiating strategy to the situation. He told the people, "Obviously you are evaluating this situation by looking at a number of things. My experience in judging people has been to consider their job-related skills, their experience, their motivation, and their personalities—how well they would fit into the organization.

"In respect of those factors, I think that I fit your needs. I have all the job-related skills you're looking for. I have the energy level to bring a lot of new things to the job. I am well-enough motivated to have reached a pretty decent salary level at a relatively early age—and even then, I don't think my last job paid me as much as I was worth. But the dollars I've earned do indicate a successful individual. In terms of personality, I feel very comfortable with the organization, and I sense that you feel comfortable with me, too. Finally, I know that I can do the job you want done."

By helping the decision along, he got the job. His argument was, "I think I'm qualified for this position, and if you agree, then I'm worth the salary you intend to pay." Had he not tailored his negotiating strategy to the specific situation, he would most likely have come in second in what, by then, had become a two-person race.

The Value of Outside Counseling

If, in your situation, negotiating an offer involves discussing many separate and complex topics, you might be well-advised to seek the counsel of an accountant, a tax or corporate lawyer, or a compensation specialist at a public accounting firm before final negotiations or after you have arranged a tentative package. Consider the subject of employment contracts, for example, which guarantee employment at certain compensation levels for a certain length of time. They have become increasingly popular in recent years, particularly at and above the upper-middle-manager level. More and more people ask for them because, in theory at least, they add security to a job. They can be two-edged swords, however. They frequently contain non-compete clauses, which may limit the individual's future employment flexibility in return for making his or her current position somewhat more secure.

Depending on how they are written, these contracts may not be much better than a more traditional handshake. On the one hand, some non-compete clauses have been overruled in court cases. On the other, since many contracts contain clauses allowing the employer to disregard their terms if the employee is fired for "cause" (unethical behavior), a slight technical irregularity can void a contract if a company is particularly unhappy with a covered employee.

At any rate, employment contracts can be intricate documents, and, if you are considering one, you should enlist a lawyer's help before signing it.

If you don't see an employment contract on your horizon, you may wish to add another negotiating item to your list. Can you expect any compensation or assistance if, six months after you accept the job, you and your employer agree that it was not a good decision? This can be tricky. An employer might wonder if you are worried about losing a job before you have taken it. But if you can show a legitimate reason to raise the issue, it is a valid bargaining point. If accepting the job means that you and your family will have to move across the country, for instance, you probably have reason to ask for some form of commitment from the company.

However important a single item may be, the ability to remain flexible will probably determine the overall acceptability of the arrangements you make. Suppose that you will have to relocate to start a new job. You ask for details of the company's relocation assistance package and learn, to your surprise, that no such thing exists. You've determined that moving your family will cost about $15,000 and you know that you simply cannot absorb that amount no matter how much you want the job.

You might say, "I suppose that you feel unable to set a precedent about relocation allowances, but I don't see how I can handle it on my own. Could you consider giving me a one-time, up-front bonus to cover the move? You wouldn't have set a precedent, it would not be a recurring expense like a salary increase, and it would let me and my family make the move without bankrupting ourselves."

Flexibility also involves knowing when to get off a subject. When you sense that you are approaching the brink on some topic, move to another. If you see hostility in someone's face, or if the company representative changes the subject abruptly, that may be a signal that there is nothing more to be said on that subject at this time. If it is a critical negotiating point, come back to it later in the meeting, perhaps acknowledging the fact that you realize you are dealing with a delicate, but important, issue.

People frequently lose job offers by over-elaborating minor points. Office space and vacation time may be important to you, but if you talk too much about them, a potential employer may decide, "This person is worrying about paper clips, and I need someone who is interested in getting the job done."

At the end of the negotiating session, it is likely that the company representative will need to refer some of your requests to his superiors. If you've brought a list of concerns with you, you might leave a copy so that nothing is missed. Then, at a subsequent meeting, you can reach final agreement on outstanding items so that you will be able to make a decision about accepting or rejecting the offer that results.

Even if all your concerns are settled immediately, however, and you are asked whether you'll accept the offer on the spot, it may be wise to wait a day or two. You could say, "I think you know how much I want this job, and I think that we've settled all the details in this session. But I'd feel much more comfortable if I took a day or two to go back over everything, just so I know I haven't neglected anything. This is a great opportunity and a very important decision for me, so I think it deserves that little extra thought."

No one should have a problem with that request. You can't ask for too much time, however. If, after weeks or months of convincing the company that you want very much to work with them, you turn around and react to a firm job offer by saying, "Fine, I'll let you know in a month," you might be considered indecisive at best and, at the worst, a little crazy. It's like a man who begs a woman to marry him and, when she finally says yes, tells her, "Great, give me a couple of weeks to think about it."

Reaching a Decision

During that one- or two-day period between receiving an offer and announcing your decision, you need to have a conversation with yourself. If you are out of work, you'll naturally want a new job. That pushes you toward accepting an offer. But how can you be certain that you've reached a good, not just an easy, decision?

Play the devil's advocate for a moment. Picture yourself losing this new job because you made a poor decision to accept it. Imagine yourself living the next few years in an unpleasant and stressful situation because you made the wrong choice. Losing your job was a difficult experience, to say the least, and it is not impossible to recreate that situation. So slow down, and convince yourself that this offer is a good one.

Good decisions end up feeling right. You won't have nagging doubts about your choice. You'll feel a sense of excitement, not just about being back at work, but about the opportunities that the new job will offer you. Finding a "perfect" job is probably impossible, but if you have been honest in creating your target and accurate in positioning this offer in terms of it, you'll make the right decision.

Don't let yourself be tripped up by dollars. Is the job a matter of fast money and fast talkers, or is it something that you can enjoy and succeed at? Refuse to tolerate a job; work at something you enjoy doing. Ten thousand dollars won't make you happy in an unbearable job, and you'll have a hard time succeeding at a job you don't enjoy.

Taking One Job to Get Another

But suppose you've been out of work for eight months, you received your last severance payment eight weeks ago, you see nothing on the horizon, and you are offered a job that seems all right but doesn't really excite you. What should you do?

After assuring yourself that there really is nothing on the horizon, you can consider the idea of taking this job to get another job. Therapeutically, it may be an excellent idea to get back to work, as long as you don't convince yourself that perhaps you'll stick with this position permanently.

Keep your search going. And don't confuse this kind of tactical move with the "brass ring" syndrome: jumping from one job to another in the blind hope that you might land somewhere interesting. By this time, you should have a pretty good idea of what "the right job" means for you. Don't settle for anything less, even if you decide to accept an interim position for personal or economic reasons.

Errors are much more likely to be made at the opposite extreme. Nine weeks after someone loses a job, he or she is offered a replacement, remains terribly upset about the entire situation, and grabs the offer just to be back at work. That happens frequently. The odds that the situation will turn out well are low.

Multiple Offers

What happens if, after you've been starving—figuratively, we hope—for eight months, your cup suddenly runneth over, and you receive two offers to choose between? That situation also occurs more frequently than most people imagine, and it gives some individuals a false sense of euphoria: "I can get two jobs now," they conclude. "Imagine what will happen if I wait another six months!" There is precious little logic to this reasoning, of course, but we've actually had to convince people to accept good jobs after they've gone six months without an offer.

If you receive two offers, refer back to your original plan once again, and try to determine how each job meets with your needs. At the outset, put questions of salary, perks, benefits, and titles out of your mind. Think about fundamental, non-negotiable things: the people you would work with at each place, the projects you would be involved with. How do the two positions weigh out against each other in these respects?

Then refer to the chart in chapter 4 and rate each job in terms of applicable criteria. This time, multiply each company value by the corresponding personal value you assigned the item. If you total the columns of numbers that result for each company, the company with the highest sum, in theory anyway, is the place that meets most of your needs.

Consider this version of the chart:

CRITERIA	My Needs	Company A		Company B		Company C	
	(1)	(2)	(1)x(2)	(3)	(1)x(3)	(4)	(1)x(4)
Decision-making Authority	6	9		6			
Size of Company	7	4		9			
Compensation base	8	9		8			
TOTAL SCORES							

Here, we have expanded the example raised earlier in this chapter so that our hypothetical job-seeker now has two offers to consider: the position at Company A, which we discussed previously, and a new offer from Company B. The individual has already determined how the criteria in the left-hand column relate to his (or her) personal needs (column 1). Decision-making authority is reasonably important to him, proper company size is somewhat crucial to his needs, and base compensation is more important still.

He has also rated the situation at Company A in terms of these same criteria (column 2). He has decided that there would be a great deal of decision-making connected to the job he has been offered there, that the size of the company is substantially different from his ideal, and that base compensation would probably be excellent at Company A.

Now he rates the opportunities at Company B (column 3). He concludes that Company B would offer slightly better-than-average opportunities for decision-making, that its size is almost ideal, and that base compensation at the company would be significantly better than normal.

How can he compare the two offers? At first glance, the job at Company A might look best, since it ranks higher than Company B for two of the three criteria. But such an interpretation of the situation would not account for the relative importance of each criterion to the individual. Company A offers more decision-making authority and higher base pay than Company B, but how important are these variables to our job-seeker? To find out, he creates a weighted value for each by multiplying the values he has awarded each company by his own needs (column 1 times column 2 and column 1 times column 3).

CRITERIA	My Needs	Company A		Company B		Company C	
	(1)	(2)	(1)x(2)	(3)	(1)x(3)	(4)	(1)x(4)
Decision-making Authority	6	9	54	6	36		
Size of Company	7	4	28	9	63		
Compensation Base	8	9	72	8	64		
TOTAL SCORES			154		163		

If the criteria are weighted to reflect the things that are most important to this individual, Company B measures up best. Its size matches his needs particularly closely, and the difference in base compensation between the two jobs is not great enough to offset this fact. While Company A offers substantially more decision-making authority than Company B, this criterion is not important enough to our job-seeker to tip the scales toward the first offer.

Particularly in its complete form (see page 81), this chart can serve as a helpful guide if you need to make a decision between more than one job offer. But it should only be used as a guide. It is only as precise as your ability to measure a variety of variables makes it. In this example, for instance, if the job-seeker had rated "Size of Company" with a 5 rather than a 7 in the "My Needs" column, the total scores would have pointed him toward Company B's offer. The full version of the chart contains enough criteria to temper the impact of an inaccurate rating, but you may be wise to refuse to determine your future on the basis of this one, admittedly mechanical, system.

In fact, while charts may help you reach a decision between two offers, you are ultimately likely to sit back, take a deep breath, and go with your gut feelings. That is often the best solution; consciously or not, you've probably been weighing the two organizations against each other all along. But being as analytical as you can as you near that decision may help a great deal.

As you think about each job, ask yourself whether you'll be able to handle its responsibilities, whether you think that you'll be successful at it, and whether you assume that you'll get along well with your new associates. How well will you interact with your new boss in each case? Where might each job take you in your career?

If, after all this thought, both offers still interest you about equally, consider going back to both companies and saying as much. If you do, be sure to announce at the start that you're not trying to inaugurate a bidding war. Give that impression, and you could lose *both* offers. No one likes to be held up. But you can try to get each company to help you decide that you should work for it.

One of our clients, with two offers to pick from, was inclined to accept one because he was not sure that he would be able to get along well with his would-be boss—the company president—at the other. We had him schedule a meeting with the president.

The two discussed the fact that they both had very different personalities, and our client came away with a clear understanding that the president considered that situation a strength rather than a weakness. He wanted our client's personality to counteract his own, and he thought that, as a result, the two would be able to work exceptionally well together.

Up to that point, our client had worried that perhaps the boss wouldn't back him in a fight. Reassured, and having felt all along that this company was preferable to the other in a number of other respects, he accepted the job.

If you think that you are about to get a second, more interesting, offer, you have fewer options. You can try to delay your response to the first company, but you have to be careful here. (Remember the marriage analogy.) If you ask for two weeks to deliberate, the offer could be withdrawn. Even if you ask for only a week, the employer might decide that you have trouble making decisions. Then, if you finally do accept the offer, you might start the job with a question mark against your name.

You might say that you need a week or two to discuss the decision with your family, particularly if the new job necessitates a move. Or you could say that you've owed your family a vacation for several years, you intend to take it now, and you'll be back in town, with an answer, in two weeks.

But be very sensitive to the employer's reaction. If you sense a chill, realize that you might jeopardize the offer by trying to delay your decision too long.

If you can earn some time from the first company, let the

second company know that you are genuinely close to making a decision about another job. You must be honest and straightforward with this because, if the second company thinks you are playing with them, they probably won't join the game.

It might be wise to say, "I feel uncomfortable bringing this up with you, and I want to assure you that it isn't a game, but I have an offer from another company, they need an answer within a week, and I would honestly like to hear from you in the meantime." Be very sensitive to what you say and how you say it in this situation.

Turning Down an Offer

When you do make your choice between two offers, or if you decide that a single offer misses your target, you need to say something more than, "No thanks," to the company you're rejecting. You've gone far enough along in the search process and shown enough interest in the job to owe the employer a simple explanation. Remember that the world, and the business world, in particular, can be a very small place.

Make a final, clean statement. Don't leave any impression that you might be bought off or that you're looking for a better offer from this company. Make a phone call and follow it with a letter. Say how difficult it was for you to reach your decision. Don't discuss specifics unless you're asked for them. Even then, try to limit your remarks to statements like, "I felt I could bring a little bit more to Company B," or, "I really appreciate the way you handled the entire selection process," or, "Your place looked awfully good to me, and it was a very tough choice."

Near Misses

Suppose the tables are turned, and, thinking that you are close to being offered a job, you find that you are instead out of the running. What happened?

It may have had nothing to do with you, so don't take it too personally. Another attractive candidate may have surfaced at the last minute. Top management could have failed to approve the position or the salary. The company might have instituted a sudden freeze on all hiring. A merger or takeover threat could have paralyzed management. Perhaps the individual you dealt with was not the actual decision-maker. Maybe someone decided that an internal promotion would be a more suitable way to fill the position. A question might even have been raised by one of your references.

Even if you are convinced that you blew things at the last moment, don't be too hard on yourself. You were probably the company's number-one or number-two choice by that late date, and someone may have decided that your competitor had a bit more experience or a slight edge in skills. None of that makes you any less worthy or valuable. But if you focus on it, it can be destructive, and you can get locked into a negative frame of mind.

Handle the situation with dignity. Leave the company's representative thinking that he or she just might have made a mistake. If you get a phone call telling you that you missed out, for instance, say, "I understand how difficult a decision that was to make." You might ask for feedback: "I'm just as interested as ever in working for a company like yours, so anything you can tell me about the way I handled myself might help me in the future." But don't press the issue. If you're told, "It was a tight race, and, in the end, we just leaned the other way," accept the explanation. Say, "Thanks for giving me the opportunity to come so close, anyway. By the way, I hope I can count on you for some ideas about other people in the industry I might talk to." What's a person going to say who has just shot you down?

Accepting an Offer

You should have no difficulty deciding what to say when you accept an offer, of course. But you may want to consider a detail or two. You may want to have conditions of your agreement put in writing, for example, not so much for protection or for legal reasons, but because it is a legitimate business concern on your part to know that nothing has fallen into a crack. Include everything from title and salary to responsibilities, reporting procedures, company cars, and relocation allowances in this document. It will clarify what will be expected of you as well as what you can expect in return. Many things have been said during the course of the selection process. Now is the time to see them in writing so that you and your new associates have no lingering misunderstandings.

Having such a memo may seem even more important to you if you've turned down an offer to accept your new job. You certainly don't want any surprises before you start work or during your first months on the job.

From the perspective of clarification, your employer should be happy to create such a document with you. It removes the chance that he will have any illusions about your new duties, too. From a legal point of view, however, he may be reluctant to commit too much to paper. If he balks, you'll simply have to decide whether you can live with the situation. If you are convinced about the job, and if you trust the people involved, then you can probably accept the slight risk that may result.

When the deal is signed and sealed, you obviously have cause for a celebration. You've weathered a major storm in your life, proving that, not only could you withstand the tempest, but you could also harness it to your advantage.

10 ∗ Starting a New Job

BEGINNING a new job is always exciting and sometimes intimidating. There is an invigorating feeling of a fresh start and a clean slate: You face new challenges and draw on a renewed sense of energy as you approach them. But you may also feel apprehensive about this new adventure. Will it actually turn out as well as you hope? You are entering a strange environment, and you must learn to work with new associates. If you were fired from your last job, you may feel particularly sensitive. "What if it happens again?" you ask yourself.

Here are ten simple suggestions that may help you make the transition to a new job more enjoyable and less stressful than you anticipate.

1. *Know yourself.* During your job search, you spent a great deal of time and energy getting to know and understand yourself. You investigated the things you do best, the things you enjoy most, and the things you'd like to do in the future. You thought about what happened at your last job.

Now that you are back at work, don't abandon that useful sense of self-interest and self-examination. Remain alert to yourself and your needs.

If you discovered that you got into trouble at your last job because you pushed people too much, too little, or in the wrong directions, remember that. When you encounter similar situations at your new job, check to see how you're acting. If you learned that you particularly enjoy solving certain kinds of problems, look for opportunities—within your sphere of responsibility—to do the same in your new position. Remember that you are likely to do best what you like best.

Many of the insights you gained during your job search are directly transferable to your new job. Don't forget them by going off to the first day of work thinking, "Whew, that's over."

2. *Set priorities.* As soon as you start work, sit down with your immediate superior to discuss priorities. As you interviewed with him, her, or other individuals during the selection process, you undoubtedly talked about a number of things that need to be done. But if you did talk to several people, they may not all have had similar thoughts on the subject, and you could have come away with an imprecise picture of what your boss thinks you should be doing at the start.

When one of our clients starts a new job, we suggest that he try to get his boss to join him in a simple exercise. The two sit down, and each makes a list of the five most important priorities he thinks the employee should attend to immediately. Typically, when the two compare their notes, they discover that they have agreed on two or three items.

If the employee starts work without going through such an exercise, he could spend 40% to 60% of his time or energy attending to duties that his superior either doesn't know about or thinks are not particularly important.

You could learn that your boss wants several small things done immediately, things he never mentioned as the two of you discussed long-term job objectives during your interviews. A major project might have been completely overlooked in the abnormal atmosphere of the selection process. He may want you to generate revenue; you may have thought he was worried about controlling costs. You pinch pennies while he hopes you're selling things.

When our company opens new offices, for instance, we've found more than once that the staff spends what we think is entirely too much time organizing things—looking at various brands of copying machines, for example, or getting the office in shape. We want them to be out knocking on doors, getting to know the companies in their area and making people aware of the services we have to offer. We get upset, they get upset, and the insidious thing about this kind of situation is that we (or your new boss) wonder why things aren't getting done, while they (or you) think that things are moving along perfectly splendidly.

Having this sort of discussion will also give you an idea of the pace your boss would like you to set at the start. You may want to jump in and show him—and everyone else—how well you can do the job. He may want you to hang back at first, study the overall picture and become familiar with the organization before making any major moves. If you don't understand each other, he may wonder what on earth you're up to.

After you compare lists, set priorities for the items on which you have both agreed. Then decide what your remaining immediate objectives should be.

3. *Study the organization's style.* If the "I Speak Your Language" personality styles proved useful during the interview phase of your search, you may find them equally helpful as you start your new job.

Consider your boss, his or her superiors, your peers, your subordinates, and even the organization as a whole. What do these people emphasize? Are they numbers-oriented? Sales-oriented? People-oriented? Are they thinkers, feelers, sensers, or intuitors? Does the organization have an overall style of its own?

Don't start a job thinking that everyone is going to

match or bend to your personality. You are the new kid on the block. You'll probably have to match the organization's style.

That doesn't mean you should try to change your personality, of course. But you may have to adapt your behavior to the company's style. Don't think of giving up any of the things that make you unique, but be sensitive to the styles of the people you're working with now. They'll be watching closely as you begin your new career.

They'll probably reach a preliminary decision about you within a month, but you'll be on parade for six months or so. Heighten your sensitivity to the "people" side of your new business during this period.

Don't allow the people at your new company to decide, "We made a poor choice. He is certainly bright enough, but he just isn't getting on the team here. He doesn't understand the way we do things."

Winning the acceptance and confidence of new associates is a building-block process. If you nourish it at the start— by being particularly sensitive to the needs of the people around you—it will get easier as you go along.

4. Listen. Don't think that you have to jump into a new job and prove yourself in the first week. Watch what is going on around you. Listen carefully. Don't make sudden moves until you understand how your new company really works.

Even if you are convinced that you know exactly what needs to be done, be careful how you act. Unless your boss has specifically told you, "Get in there and clean out that nest of snakes by Tuesday," move cautiously. You won't cement a good working relationship with superiors or peers, not to mention subordinates, if you are labeled a know-it-all.

Don't make statements like, "Well, at [your former company], we did it this way." Don't suggest to people at your new company that things are done better somewhere else. Even if that is true, why give the credit to your former employer, anyway? Make the suggestion your own idea: "I wonder if this might work?"

5. *Do small things well.* While it is unwise to initiate major projects when you first join a company, you don't have to sit around and drink in the atmosphere of the place for your first six months on the job. You can show how responsive you can be, how well you attend to details, how disciplined you are and how willing you are to accept unglamorous but necessary projects if you start your new career by doing small things quickly and well.

We are particularly well-acquainted with one man who may have assured himself a successful career with a major foods corporation by being able to tag meat. It wasn't in his job description, and he had no experience organizing food lockers, but soon after he joined the company, his new boss asked him to make some sense out of a freezer-room full of meat.

Our friend said, "Fine," put on a heavy coat, went into the storage room, and devised a system of color-coded, dated tags that showed which type of meat had arrived at the facility on which date.

When he returned to his office and told his boss what he'd done, he wasn't prepared for the response. His superior was overjoyed. Our friend didn't understand all the jubilation, but he didn't mind it, either. The freezer room had obviously been a thorn in his boss's side for some time. The boss concluded that his new employee was the brightest guy to come along in years.

You don't have to go out and save humanity in your first month on the job to earn yourself a solid reputation.

6. *Don't knock your former employer.* You refrained from hurling invective at your former employer throughout your job search. Don't give in to the impulse now. First, no one at your new company is likely to be interested. Second, those who are may wonder whether you might describe them in the same terms in the future. Others may ask if you ever got over leaving your last job. They may worry, and rightfully so, that a preoccupation with the past could cut into your current effectiveness.

If you are asked about your former employer, say, "It was a great place. After all, it got me here, didn't it?"

7. *Learn what happened to your predecessor.* During the interview process, you should have determined how your new position became available. If you didn't, look for that information now. What happened to your predecessor? If he was promoted or moved elsewhere within the company, he may be able to provide valuable information about the job. If he was fired, what went wrong? What should you do differently?

Even if you did cover this ground during an interview, it won't hurt to ask again. You're an insider now, and you may get an insider's answer that is markedly different from a response offered for public consumption. Or, you may get the same answer but be able to interpret it from your new, insider's perspective.

Don't approach this information thinking that if the person who last held the job got fired, the odds are greater than normal that you will be fired. Don't assume that if you were fired from your last job, you have a better than average chance of getting fired again. Use what you've learned to determine what it will take to be a success in this job, not to learn what you'll have to do to keep from losing it.

8. *Transform warning signals into guidelines.* Refer back to the seven danger signs which, as we said in chapter one, show that a job is not secure. Each can be turned around and made into a positive guideline for successful employment. Remain aware of them in this optimistic context from your first day on the job.

You may recall that the first, and most important, warning sign is the feeling that you hate your job. As you start your new job, refuse to abdicate responsibility for yourself. Instead of avoiding the subject, make it a continuing concern to monitor your satisfaction with your job. If you begin to sense displeasure, you'll be able to do something about it. At the very least, you'll be in a position to act and not be acted upon.

Rather than discover at some future time that you have

"lost your voice" at the company, dedicate yourself to creating effective communications and good visibility at your new job.

Don't hide from feedback or wait passively for negative reports from peers or superiors. Actively seek out comments from the people around you. By doing so, you'll not only show how seriously you take your job, you'll also be able to correct minor issues so that major problems do not develop.

Look at all seven warning signs and figure out how you can turn them to your advantage so that you are never surprised by them.

9. *Respect your peers and subordinates.* When you start a new job, deal as conscientiously with your peers and subordinates as you do with your superiors. The people who work for you, after all, are the individuals who can make you great. Deal with the "people" side of your business before you immerse yourself in business decisions.

You may run into disagreement on this subject at some companies. There are still places ruled by hard-nosed, "Get it done and don't worry about the human consequences" types. Thankfully, however, business seems to be moving toward more participative management styles.

If you start a job assuming that you are the "BOSS," basing your belief on whatever may be written in your job description, you're probably in for a surprise, and not a happy one. Subordinates no longer leap automatically to carry out the wishes of their bosses. Blind allegiance is not a growth industry these days. You need to earn the respect of the people you work with before they'll make you look great.

10. *Enjoy yourself.* This is so obvious that it should be called an axiom or premise rather than a suggestion. But, for many people, reorganizing a faltering division, introducing a new product, or doubling sales is child's play compared to actually entertaining the thought that they have a right to enjoy their work.

All jobs involve some bad days and unpleasant duties. But, beginning with day one, if you cannot sit back at any time and reflect honestly that, overall, you are happy with what you've done and are doing, you may not really be able to consider yourself a success.

Ultimately, this book is not about leaving one job or finding another. Its subject is much more general: understanding and attaining job security and career satisfaction. In the final analysis, both may have little to do with any specific job. The world is too uncertain a place, and your needs may change too rapidly, for a single job to satisfy you permanently. If you try to arrange your life in that manner, you may put the cart before the horse. You need to place yourself ahead of, and above, any particular job.

You deserve to enjoy your new job, of course. And if you are guided by personal satisfaction and strengthened by professional competence, this job is almost certain to bring you greater rewards than you've ever enjoyed in the past.

But consider an even greater reward: the comfortable knowledge that you are doing exactly what you want to do. Let your real job be a determination to learn about and listen to yourself so that, in this job and in any that may follow it, you control your career and future, and refuse to settle for anything less.

Appendix

JOB-SEARCH RESOURCES

Some or all of the following directories may be useful to you in planning your marketing strategy. These directories, and many others, can be found at local business, college, or university libraries.

Before using any directory, read its preface and table of contents. This simple procedure will save you countless hours and show you the most efficient way to locate the information you need.

Directory of Executive Recruiters. Consultants News, Templeton Road, Fitzwilliam, N.H. 03447.

A listing of over 2,300 recruiter offices in the U.S., Canada, and Mexico. Cross-indexed.

Guide to American Directories. B. Klein Publications, P.O. Box 8503, Coral Springs, Florida 33065. 567 pages.

A listing and description of 6,000 directories with over 300 major industrial, professional, and mercantile classifications. Useful in locating membership names and titles.

Encyclopedia of Associations. Volume 1. National Organizations of the United States, Gale Research Company, Book Tower, Detroit, Michigan 48266. 1,465 pages.

A guide to 14,000 national and international organizations of all types, purposes, and interests. Gives names and headquarters addresses, telephone numbers, chief officials, number of members, staffs and chapters, descriptions of membership, programs and activities. Includes list of special committees and departments, publications, and a three-year convention schedule. Cross-indexed. Useful in locating placement committees at major trade organizations which can help you learn of specific job openings in your field of interest; getting membership lists of individuals in order to develop personal contacts; learning where and when conferences are being held so that you can attend them and develop personal contacts and position leads.

Standard and Poor's Register of Corporations, Directors and Executives. 3 volumes. 345 Hudson Street, New York, New York 10014.

A guide to the business community providing information on public companies in the United States.

Volume 1, Corporate Listings. 2,419 pages.

Alphabetical listing by business name of 37,000 corporations, including addresses, telephone numbers, names, titles of officers and directors, public firms (SIC) Standard Industrial Classification codes (for company/industry cross-referencing), annual sales, number of employees, some division names, principal and secondary businesses.

Volume II, Directors and Executives. 1,600 pages.

Alphabetical list of 75,000 individuals serving as officers, directors, trustees, partners, etc. and their principal business affiliations, with official titles and business and residence addresses. Where obtainable, year and place of birth, college, year of graduation, and fraternal memberships are listed.

Volume III, Indexes. 805 pages.

Divided into six color-coded sections:

Section 1 (Green). *Standard Industrial Classification Index* (SIC).

Section 2 (Pink). *Standard Industrial Classification Codes.*

Provides a defined breakdown according to a company's line of business.

Section 3 (Buff). *Geographic Index.*

Lists companies in the *Register* by state and major cities. Business names are alphabetical.

Section 4 (Green). *Obituary Section.*

Records of deaths in past year of individuals; provides their affiliations, business addresses, and dates of birth.

Section 5 (Blue). *New Individual Additions.*

Alphabetical list of individuals appearing in the *Register* for the first time, with their principal business connections and business addresses.

Section 6 (Blue). *New Company Additions.*

Alphabetical list of companies appearing in the *Register* for the first time; supplies their business addresses.

Standard and Poor's Register Supplement (Quarterly).

Updating of data for the above volumes.

Dun & Bradstreet Million Dollar Directory. Volume 1. Dun & Bradstreet, Inc., 99 Church Street, New York, New York 10007. 5,082 pages.

Similar to *Standard and Poor's Register,* but limits itself to corporations with sales of $1 million or above. It is useful to use the two together. One directory may include a firm the other does not mention, and either may describe products, subsidiaries, and offer titles that the other neglects.

Dun & Bradstreet Million Dollar Directory. Volume II, The Middle Market. 3,727 pages.

Includes companies whose net worth is $500,000 to $999,999.

Dun & Bradstreet Reference Book of Corporate Managements. 1,430 pages.

Contains data on directors and selected officers of 2,400 companies with annual sales of $20 million or more and/or 1,000 or more employees. Information includes dates of birth, education, and business positions presently and previously held. For directors who are not officers, present principal business connections are supplied. Gives details of corporate officers not available in the above directories, and some idea of the personality of a corporation by providing information on the technical background of its officers.

Directory of Corporate Affiliations. National Register Publishing Co. Inc., 5201 Old Orchard Road, Skokie, Illinois 60076.

Provides detailed information on "who runs what" as a result of mergers and acquisitions. Contains companies listed on the New York Stock Exchange, the American Stock Exchange, the "Fortune 500" and others, totaling 4,000 listings of parent companies. Helps determine the detailed corporate structure of a parent company and identifies companies not listed in other directories above because they are subsidiary divisions or affiliates.

Standard Directory of Advertisers and Supplements. National Register Publishing Company, Inc. 1,122 pages.

Lists 17,000 companies doing national and regional advertising, with names, telephone numbers, products, or services; 80,000 executives and their titles with the advertising agency handling each account, account executives, time and amount of appropriation, media used, and distribution. Companies are listed by product classification, alphabetically, and by trade name. A useful tool in locating marketing officers, names of parent companies, subsidiaries and affiliates. A known trade name can be used to locate the manufacturer.

Standard Directory of Advertising Agencies. National Register Publishing Company, Inc. 900 pages.

Lists a total of 4,400 agency establishments, 4,000 U.S. and 400 foreign.

Thomas Register of American Manufacturers. Thomas Publishing Company, One Penn Plaza, New York, New York 10001. 12 volumes.

Useful in locating many specific product manufacturers, both large and small, not listed in any of the other directories.

Volumes 1–7. Products and services listed alphabetically. Brand names and index in Volume 7.

Volume 8. Company names, addresses, and telephone numbers listed alphabetically with branch offices, capital ratings, and company officials.

Volumes 9–12. Catalogues of companies listed alphabetically and cross-indexed in the first 8 volumes.

Polk's World Bank Directory. North American Edition (U.S., Canada, Mexico, Central America, Caribbean). R. L. Polk Company, 2001 Elm Hill Pike, P.O. Box 1340, Nashville, Tennessee 37202.

A major detailed directory listing banks and other financial institutions and government agencies by address; includes geographic indexing, with maps, names, and titles of officers. Useful for corporations and government agencies.

Best's Insurance Reports, Property and Casualty. A. M. Best Company, Ambest Road, Oldwick, New Jersey 08858. 1,800 pages.

Gives in-depth analyses, operating statistics, financial data, and officers of over 1,300 major stock and mutual property-casualty insurance companies. Provides summary data on over 2,000 smaller mutual companies and on 300 casualty companies operating in Canada.

Best's Insurance Reports, Life and Health. 2,000 pages.

Supplies 1,250 individual company reports in addition to summaries of 600 smaller companies similar to the property and casualty reports.